COVENTRY BUSES
1948–1974

DAVID HARVEY

AMBERLEY

31 (GKV 31)

Front Cover Bottom: The first of the GKV-registered, Metro-Cammell-bodied Daimler CVA6s was 31 (GKV 31). This bus was delivered in November 1948, despite the registration letters being reserved during the previous March. The bus is in Broadgate in 1960 and has just pulled away from the temporary bus stops in the shadow of Holy Trinity church. It is starting its journey on the 22 route to Willenhall to the east of the city, which initially ran from Broadgate to Purcell Road off Sewall Highway and was introduced in January 1955. (M. Rooum)

207 (SKV 207)

Front Cover Top: In April 1967 Daimler CVG6 bus 207 (SKV 207) has turned off Fairfax Street into Pool Meadow, which was being rebuilt at this time. The MCCW-bodied sixty-seater bus is working on the 8 route from Tile Hill Village, a service that had an 8-minute headway. On this pleasantly sunny day, customers are sitting outside The Beech Tree Café, which was opposite the original 1930s Tudor-styled Meadow Café. The advert carried on the between decks offside panelling of the Metro-Cammell bodywork is for Monk's Sausages and Pies, which was only applied to three other Coventry Transport buses. (M. S. Gunn)

338 (CDU 338B)

Rear Cover: Leyland and Daimler had both developed rear-engined double-deckers with the former producing the Atlantean as a production vehicle in 1958 and Daimler getting their Fleetline into production in 1962. The choice for Coventry was obvious, to support local industry, but the first order for the new breed of Coventry bus caused a political outcry when the order went to Leyland as the Daimler Radford Works was in the city. 338 (CDU 338B) was the first of the twenty-two Leyland Atlantean PDR1/2s with Willowbrook H44/32F bodywork delivered in January 1965. It sits outside Burton's outfitters in Broadgate when operating on the 21 service to Wood End. (A. J. Douglas)

First published 2015

Amberley Publishing
The Hill, Stroud
Gloucestershire, GL5 4EP

www.amberley-books.com

British Library Cataloguing in Publication Data.
A catalogue record for this book is available from the British Library.

ISBN 978 1 4456 5178 1 (print)
ISBN 978 1 4456 5179 8 (ebook)

Typeset in 10pt on 13pt Sabon.
Typesetting and Origination by Amberley Publishing.
Printed in the UK.

Contents

Acknowledgements

The author is grateful to the many photographers acknowledged in the text who have contributed to this volume. I sincerely thank all of those who are still alive for allowing me to use pictures, many of which were taken more than sixty years ago. Thanks are also due to the late A. A. Cooper, Bob Mack, Roy Marshall and Alf Owen, who all printed photographs for me many years ago and generously gave permission for me to use their material. Thanks are also due to Alistar Douglas, Ray Wilson and Fred York. Where the photographer is not known, the photographs are credited to my own collection. The route maps were produced by the author. Special thanks are due to my wife Diana for her splendid proof reading.

The book would not have been possible without the continued encouragement given by Louis Archard at Amberley Publishing.

Bibliography

Bailey, Roger, *Coventry Transport 1884–1940* (Tempus, 2006).
Bailey, Roger, *Coventry Transport 1940–1974* (Tempus, 2007).
Brush Coachwork body lists Parts 1B, 2 and 3 (PSV Circle BB 279–281).
Coventry A–Z Street Map (Geographers' A–Z Maps).
Coventry Corporation Transport (PSV Circle PD2, 1974).
Coventry Corporation Transport Society website, http://cct-society.org.uk/index.html
Coventry Transport 1912–1974: A commemorative brochure.
Daimler Chassis List 1928–1941 (PSV Circle C1200, 2009).
Daimler Chassis List 11304–16684 (PSV Circle C1201, 2010).
Denton, A. S. and F. P. Groves, *Coventry Transport 1884–1940 Part One* (BTHG, 1985).
Denton, A. S. and F. P. Groves, *Coventry Transport 1940–1974 Part Two* (BTHG, 1987).
Douglas, A., *Memories of Coventry* (Coventry Newspapers, 1987).
Guy Chassis List Heavy Series 22000–38437 (PSV Circle C1300, 2013).
McGrory, D., *Coventry at War in Old Photographs* (Sutton, 1997).
Metro-Cammell Body List 1936–1943 (PSV Circle BB252, 1992).
Old Ordnance Survey Maps; Coventry 1905 (1996).
Pevsner, N., *Buildings of England BE31: Warwickshire* (Penguin, 1966).
Smith, A. and D. Fry, *The Coventry We Have Lost* (1991).

Introduction

This is the second part of a two-volume work on the buses operated by Coventry Transport. This book covers the period from the end of the Second World War, beginning with the first post-war buses delivered in April 1948, only twenty-five months after the last of the wartime buses had entered service. The book continues from the first post-war half-cab, exposed radiator buses to the first buses fitted with 'New Look' concealed radiators, which were also the last 'heavyweight' buses of the R. A. Fearnley period of management. The second period of bus standardisation lasted from 1955 until 1963 when no fewer than 170 Daimler CVG6s with lightweight, high-capacity Metro-Cammell bodies were purchased. These buses caused the withdrawal of all the pre-war and wartime buses from the streets of Coventry, the last one finally going in 1964. Throughout the post-war years Coventry Transport had a small fleet of single-deckers for private hire work, but gradually the need for single-deckers was eliminated, though the only coach taken into PTE ownership from a municipality came from the Coventry Transport fleet. From 1965, after a brief, if controversial, purchase of twenty-two Leyland Atlanteans, the rear-engined Daimler Fleetline was exclusively the double-decker of choice and buses ordered by the Transport Department were delivered to West Midlands PTE for almost four years after the take-over date. Fortunately several buses from the era covered by this volume have survived into preservation.

The post-war years, after the wartime hiatus of replacing the hastily abandoned tram routes, saw a gradual increase in the number of routes, which eventually numbered twenty-three though there were numerous additions and branches in the outer suburbs, resulting in these variations getting an A suffix letter. This resulted in the bus fleet increasing in size from 263 in 1945 to a maximum of 333 in 1960. When the PTE took over on 1 April 1974, 308 buses were taken over.

All, however, was not well as although the mileages operated had gone up by 25 per cent to 9.78 million by 1965, passenger numbers which had peaked at just over 110 million in 1950 were declining rapidly so that by 1973 barely 63 million passengers were carried during that financial year. This meant that an annual profit of £57,500 in 1960 had become an operating loss of £37,600 in the last operating financial year. So although municipal bus operation in Coventry was always kept to the highest standards, it was not perhaps too surprising that the takeover was met without too much internal resistance after the boundaries of the West Midlands County Council were extended to include Coventry.

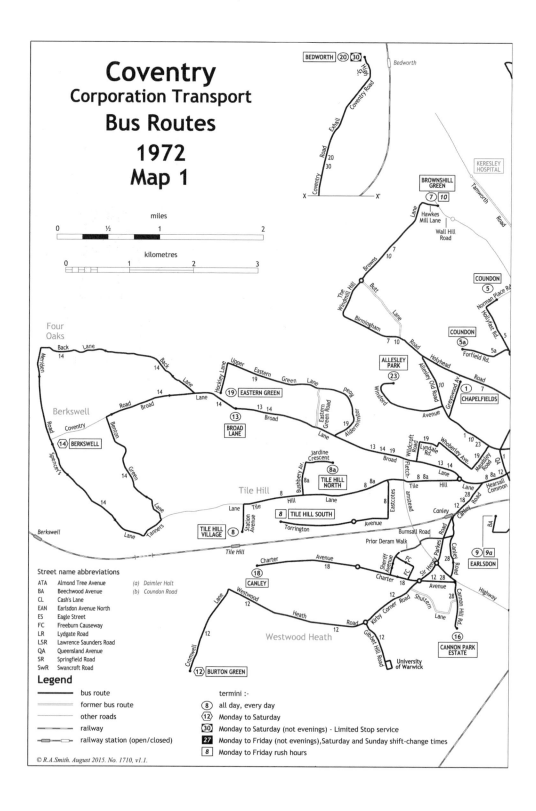

Coventry
Corporation Transport
Bus Routes
1972
Map 1

miles

0   ½   1   2

kilometres

0   1   2   3

Four Oaks

Berkswell

Tile Hill

Westwood Heath

Street name abbreviations

ATA	Almond Tree Avenue
BA	Beechwood Avenue
CL	Cash's Lane
EAN	Earlsdon Avenue North
ES	Eagle Street
FC	Freeburn Causeway
LR	Lydgate Road
LSR	Lawrence Saunders Road
QA	Queensland Avenue
SR	Springfield Road
SwR	Swancroft Road

(a) Daimler Halt
(b) Coundon Road

Legend

▬▬▬	bus route
══	former bus route
──	other roads
▬▬▬	railway
▭◁▷▭	railway station (open/closed)

termini :-

⑧	all day, every day
⑫	Monday to Saturday
㉚	Monday to Saturday (not evenings) - Limited Stop service
27	Monday to Friday (not evenings),Saturday and Sunday shift-change times
8	Monday to Friday rush hours

© R.A.Smith. August 2015. No. 1710, v1.1.

BEDWORTH ⑳ ㉚   Bedworth

KERESLEY HOSPITAL

BROWNSHILL GREEN ⑦ ⑩

Hawkes Mill Lane

Wall Hill Road

COUNDON ⑤

COUNDON ⑤ₐ

Forfield Rd.

ALLESLEY PARK ㉓

CHAPELFIELDS ① ⑦

EASTERN GREEN ⑲

BROAD LANE ⑬

BERKSWELL ⑭

Jardine Crescent ⑧ₐ

TILE HILL NORTH

TILE HILL SOUTH ⑧

TILE HILL VILLAGE ⑧

EARLSDON ⑨ ⑨ₐ

CANNON PARK ESTATE ⑯

University of Warwick

CANLEY ⑱

BURTON GREEN ⑫

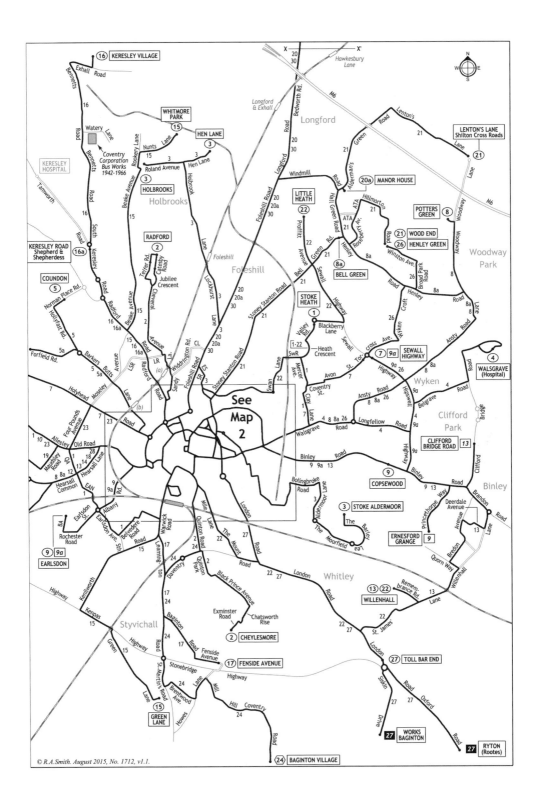

© R.A.Smith. August 2015, No. 1712, v1.1.

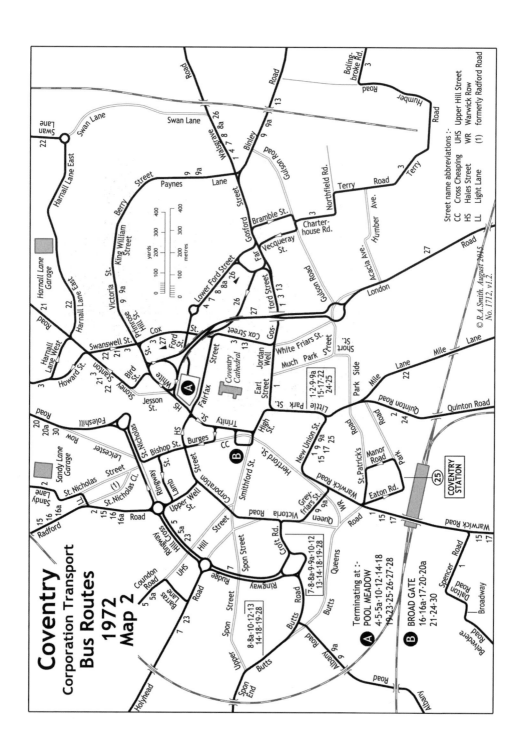

Coventry
Corporation Transport
Bus Routes
1972
Map 2

Terminating at :-

A POOL MEADOW
4·5·5a·10·12·14·18
19·23·25·26·27·28

B BROAD GATE
16·16a·17·20·20a
21·24·30

Street name abbreviations :-
CC Cross Cheaping   UHS Upper Hill Street
HS Hales Street   WR   Warwick Row
LL Light Lane   (1)   formerly Radford Road

© R.A.Smith, August 2015
No. 1712, v1.2.

Early Post-War Buses

GNE 247

The prototype Crossley double-decker arrived in Coventry in 1946 and worked the Walsgrave service to demonstrate the Brockhouse-Salerni automatic torque-convertor gearbox. The result of this demonstration led to the much later token order for bus number 100 (GKV 100). When this first post-war Crossley was built in March 1944, all was ready. Manchester Corporation's Crossley Mancunian 1211 was taken out of service and its body removed at Gorton by Crossleys. It was then fitted to the new chassis, designated DD42/1 (meaning Double-deck, 4 wheels, 2 driven, Mark 1). The new bus entered service on May Day 1944, registered GNE 247, carrying the Manchester fleet number 1217 despite still being owned by Crossley. It had a newly designed tall radiator with straight sides and a quite high bonnet line. There was the new direct-injection 8.6 litre HOE7 (Heavy Oil Engine type 7), which, due to hurried redesigning due to patent infringements, caused serious problems with the engine, specifically very poor airflows in the cylinder head, blowing head gaskets and back pressure causing cylinder head crack damage, poor fuel economy and a propensity to leak engine oil. Crossley resurrected Leyland's pre-war concept of the torque converter, calling it the 'Turbo Transmitter'. It was built by Brockhouse-Salerni and the improvements included a fully automatic change to direct drive for which the driver did not need to select. Unfortunately it was neither simple to maintain or reliable. The new body intended for 1217 was completed eight months later and fitted to the chassis of 1211, re-entering service in December 1944. After being trialled in Manchester it was quietly demonstrated in the months after the end of the war and as Crossley Motors had spare construction capacity for both chassis and bodies, orders quickly came in and frequently not long after their arrival, orders for further new buses went to other manufacturers due to reliability problems. It is seen parked in central Manchester when renumbered 2960. (R. F. Mack)

1 (FHP 1)

The new post-war buses comprised a huge order for ninety-six Daimler CVA6s which had been placed in the summer of 1945. Unlike the pre-war fleet, all the post-war half-cab double-deck bodies until the autumn of 1963 were built by Metro-Cammell. The first post-war Coventry Transport bus was 1 (FHP 1), which was delivered to the undertaking in April 1948. It is standing in Broadgate with Priory Row's timber-framed, seventeenth-century buildings in the background to the right of the bus. The first post-war order was for thirty double-deckers consisting of twenty-eight Daimler CVA6s with Metro-Cammell H31/29R bodies and one Daimler CVD6 and an AEC Regent III. The CVA6s were intended to have been fitted with specially designed bodies based on the style of the lightweight 1939/40 Metro-Cammell-built Daimler COA/60s, 234–237, but Metro-Cammell would only accept orders from their standardised types of bodies. Coventry therefore accepted the general body design built for Birmingham City Transport. These were ordered in February 1946 but deliveries only began with this bus in April 1948, even though the chassis had been completed in August 1947! The complete Metro-Cammell-bodied Daimler CVA6s weighed a surprisingly heavy 7 tons 17 cwt. Bus 1 remained in service until March 1966. It is working on the 21 service to Coventry railway station. (S. N. J. White)

2 (FHP 2)

The deep Beclawat 12-inch-deep sliding saloon windows disguised the fact that the Metro-Cammell bodies delivered to Coventry Transport on the Daimler CVA6s were modified versions of the bodies delivered to Birmingham City Transport on their GOE-registered Daimler CVG6. A two-landing staircase was standard and allowed extra seats to be fitted into the lower saloon. 2 (FHP 2) stands near to Sandy Lane garage in company with the later 'New Look' front 158 (KVC 158) in about 1955 as FHP 2 has a SAY CWS AND SAVE advertisement, which was common throughout the mid-1950s. (D. F. Parker)

3 (FHP 3)

Opposite: After its withdrawal in the spring of 1966, 3 (FHP 3) was sold to Priory Coaches of Leamington, who ran the bus from May 1966 until March 1969. The bus is in Priory Coaches' blue and white livery and looks in quite good, albeit somewhat worn, condition. It is parked at Drayton Manor Park when working on a school trip in June 1967. The AEC A173 7.58 litre-engined Daimler could easily be distinguished by the pair of round apertures in the side of the bonnet in order to access the oil filler cap and dip stick without having to open the whole bonnet assembly. (N. D. Griffiths)

6 (FHP 6)

Above: The washing is drying on the line of the house overlooking the empty bus as the bus crew stands in front of their vehicle at the Lenton's Lane terminus of the 6 route in the north-east of the city. The bus is 6 (FHP 6). The 6 route reached Lenton's Lane by way of Alderman's Green in October 1937 and terminated just beyond the Old Crown public house, adjacent to the 1920s municipal houses built at the western end of Lenton's Lane. This Daimler CVA6 had entered service in June 1948 and was sold to W. T. Bird of Stratford in February 1965 and was broken up. The bus is wearing an advertisement for the Northampton-based Phipps brewery, who somewhat surprisingly only had one tied-pub in Coventry. (C. W. Routh)

9 (FHP 9)

Above: Although looking a quite standard Metro-Cammell-bodied Daimler CVA6, 9 (FHP 9) had been badly damaged when in a collision with a railway bridge on 7 January 1956 the roof was completely sliced off! It was sent to Metro-Cammell's Elmdon factory a fortnight later and was fitted with a new top deck to the original design. Some years before this dramatic event, 9 has travelled along Binley Road and stands at the bus shelters at the Copsewood terminus at Bromleigh Drive when new in 1948. This bus would remain in service until February 1966 and was sold along with ten other CVA6s to one George Hilditch, an early post-war dealer in buses and coaches who was based in Benton Green, Coventry. (D. R. Harvey Collection)

11 (FHP 11)

Opposite below: 'A field of recently planted Coventry buses!' In reality there are seven former Corporation buses standing derelict and awaiting scrapping at Bird's scrapyard in Stratford-upon-Avon. Withdrawn buses would be driven from Coventry under their own power and the best ones parked on Bird's forecourt alongside Birmingham Road as prospective second-hand sales vehicles. If they hadn't been snapped up, then they would make the one-way journey down into the old brick quarry where these buses are languishing. Metro-Cammell-bodied Daimler CVA6s 11 (FHP 11), 91 (GKV 91) and two others, plus Maudslay Regent IIIs 119, 120 and 125, stand in the mud as they await their imminent doom! (R. Saward)

10 (FHP 10)

Above: Travelling behind an Austin 12 first registered in August 1949 is MCCW-bodied Daimler CVA6 10 (FHP 10), which is working on the 11 route to Binley. The car's driver is doing a hand signal while the bus has just passed the early nineteenth-century retail premises that are due to be demolished as part of the redevelopment of the area just outside the city centre. Osborne's newsagent and tobacconist shop, with rows of magazines pegged up over the window in a style more redolent of the left bank of the River Seine in Paris than Coventry, has a huge sign for Woodbine cigarettes, which perversely were very cheap and very small! (R. F. Mack)

Above: **18 (FHP 18)**

Passing the Council House in Earl Street is 18 (FHP 18). This AEC-engined Daimler has come into the city from Willenhall when working on the 11 route to Glendown Avenue, a service introduced during March 1932. The CVA6 model had an AEC A173 7.58-litre direct-injection engine with flexible engine mountings which, when coupled to the unladen weight of 7 tons 10cwt 2 qtrs of the Metro-Cammell body, managed to give a surprisingly comfortable ride and a good performance, although with a full load of sixty passengers it could become more on the stately side of brisk! The Tudor-styled Council House was completed in 1920 and was built in red sandstone with mullioned windows and bay windows on the first floor. (R. F. Mack)

23 (FHP 23)

Opposite below: Carrying the Drinka Pinta Milka Day advertisement introduced by the Milk Marketing Board in 1959 is 23 (FHP 23), a Daimler CVA6 with the usual MCCW H31/29R bodywork that had entered service in November 1948. The bus, with its brightly polished chromed radiator, is working on the 16A service to Green Lane in about 1960. It is preparing to pull away from the bus stop in Warwick Road at the railway bridge near to Coventry station and appears to be loaded up with nearly its full complement of sixty passengers. 23 was to remain in service until the spring of 1966 as one of the last of the 1948-built buses to survive in service. (R. Marshall)

26 (FHP 26)

Above: About to enter Pool Meadow bus station is Daimler CVA6 FHP 26. Just as in nearby Birmingham, Coventry Transport buses frequently used the somewhat unhelpful SERVICE EXTRA destination, though, as in this case, the final destination was often shown. 26 entered service in September 1948 and the Metro-Cammell body still retained its Birmingham heritage with an angled windscreen designed to prevent reflections from the lower saloon at night and the thick corner pillars to the front of the upper saloon. Yet the multitude of deep opening windows in each saloon, the half-turn staircase, the jelly-mould saloon light covers and much plainer upholstery all purported to alter the appearance of these exposed radiator buses. (R. H. G. Simpson)

29 (FHP 29)

Waiting at the top of Trinity Street to continue its journey to Baginton Village on the 17 route is a still fairly new 29 (FHP 29). The chassis of this bus, numbered 13434, was the last of the initial tranche of Daimler CVD6s ordered by Coventry in February 1946, but it only arrived in November 1948. The building with the jettied half-timbered frontage and large bay windows behind the bus looks Tudor but was actually built in 1938 to blend in with the genuine early fifteenth-century Lych Gate Cottages buildings beyond the steps to the right in Priory Row. For many years these were the premises of Timothy White's, the chemist, but today it is a Wetherspoon's public house called The Flying Standard. (W. J. Haynes)

33 (GKV 33)

Parked in Broadgate outside Salisbury's handbag shop is 33 (GKV 33). Behind the bus is the upper end of The Precinct and the lower storeys of the Leofric Hotel, which was opened in 1955 as part of the massive post-war redevelopment scheme. The Precinct was built on the line of Smithford Street, which was totally destroyed on the night of 14/15 November 1940. The bus is being used on the 16A service to Keresley on a warm day judging by the number of windows opened in the upper saloon. The bus was one of seventeen Metro-Cammell-bodied Daimler CVA6s that entered service in November 1948. (M. Hayhoe)

40 (GKV 40)

The Carl Rosa Operatic Chorus was appearing at the Coventry Hippodrome Theatre in about 1951 when the rather well-loaded Daimler CVA6, 40 (GKV40), operating on the 7 route to Sewell Highway, was standing at the bus stop in Hales Street. The German opera and chorus company, which sang German, French and Italian opera in English, was founded in 1873 by Carl August Rosa, who was a music impresario whose aim was to present well-known opera stars leading a company of new artistes and regularly appeared at Coventry. Also appearing in a separate show was Big Bill Campbell and his Rocky Mountain Rhythm, who played Country & Western music in this country from the 1930s until the early 1950s. Bill Campbell was a Canadian whose real name was Clarence Church Campbell, but he also appeared as Zeke Winters. (D. R. Harvey Collection)

42 (GKV 42)
A 'different'-looking Metro-Cammell-bodied Daimler CVA6 was 42 (GKV 42). This bus had hopper ventilators in the upper saloon front windows. These looked like a throwback to the ventilators on the wartime deliveries, but somehow appeared out of place on these post-war buses. The bus is parked alongside the rudimentary bus shelters in the lay-by in front of the Herbert Library Art Gallery in Jordan Well when working on the 1 route to Stoke Heath. Behind the bus is the Council House built during the First World War and the medieval tower of the original Coventry Cathedral. (Vectis)

44 (GKV 44)

Standing outside Frederick Wright's splendid display of different brands of tobacco in his Cross Cheaping shop window in 1951 is 44 (GKV 44). This almost new Metro-Cammell-bodied Daimler CVA6 is being used on the 20 route to Bedworth. This bus route was introduced in November 1940 to replace the tram service 1 to Bedworth after the surviving tram routes were abandoned because of air raid damage. Behind bus 44 is 327 (EKV 327), an un-rebuilt wartime Weymann-bodied Guy Arab II bus which would be rebuilt by Nudd Brother & Lockyer later during the same year. (R. Wilson)

46 (GKV 46)

There is something about the private houses built in Coventry's enlarging suburbia in the 1920s which is strangely distinctive. They were frequently built in a small terrace with large, often mullioned, bay windows on both storeys and a small mock Tudor faced gable above each bay – a characteristic of many of the houses in the city of this age. Such houses are behind the turning bus, which is returning to Harnall Lane via Keresley. The bus is 46 (GKV 46), a Daimler CVA6 with a Metro-Cammell H31/29R body which had entered service in December 1948. Behind it, working on the 16 service to Green Lane, is bus 279 (XVC 279), a Daimler CVG6 with an Orion type lightweight Metro-Cammell body delivered in October 1959. (R. F. Mack)

52 (GKV 52)

Opposite: The nearly-new Daimler CVA6 52 (GKV 52) stands in Eaton Road near to Coventry railway station when working on the 6 route to Bell Green. The rear end of the Metro-Cammell bodywork on the early post-war Coventry Transport buses was to the Birmingham City Transport design but with modifications to suit both the undertaking's specifications and passengers' modesty. On the rear platform the half-turn staircase enabled its intrusion into both saloons to be minimised, especially downstairs where, with the use of a rear-facing five-seat bench across the front bulkhead, twenty-nine passengers could be squeezed inside. The staircase arrangement necessitated the use of a pair of small platform windows which gave the rear of these buses an idiosyncratic and slightly homemade appearance. This was one of the buses that were fitted with a clear offside platform window when new. This soon caused complaints to be received as it did little to protect the modesty of women climbing the stairs when wearing skirts. Belfast Corporation addressed the problem of female modesty by having the rear platform window made with a half clear and a half frosted pane, but soon after delivery the offside window on Coventry's buses was fitted with a dark tinted pane which was repeated on the side staircase window. (R. Wilson)

55 (GKV 55)

Above: 'Old buses never die; they just become driver trainers in the service fleet.' Three of Coventry Transport's Metro-Cammell-bodied Daimler CVA6s, 55 (GKV 55), with service fleet number 06, 19 (FHP 19) as 00 and 69 (GKV 69) as 09, all stand in Harnall Lane garage yard. The three buses were withdrawn in 1966 but not before FHP 19 was renumbered 419 during the year that it was taken out of passenger service. These buses were, in August 1966, placed into the driving school fleet of tuition buses and fitted with large radiator signs displaying a large red letter L and the legend 'DRIVER UNDER INSTRUCTION'. At least two of the buses have the mid-1960s livery variation introduced by Mr Noel McDonald, the new General Manager, with the municipal crest placed slightly lower with the fleet name above it in small upper case lettering. Buses 55, 19 and 69 survived as trainers until March 1969, August 1968 and September 1969 respectively. (R. H. G. Simpson)

60 (GKV 60)

Above: On 13 March 1959 Daimler CVA6 60 (GKV 60) passes St George's church in Barker's Butts Lane on the corner of Banks Street. The Metro-Cammell-bodied sixty-seater is working on the 5A service towards Coventry Rugby Union Club's Coundon Road ground and has a bulkhead slipboard showing Kingsbury Road, which was at the outer terminus at the western end of Forfield Road in Coundon, a residential suburb to the north-west of the city. St George's church was dedicated in 1939, not long after the surrounding semi-detached housing. It was built in an art deco-detailed Perpendicular style in red brick and has a distinctive west tower with a low octagonal second stage surmounted by a spire. The entrance to the church is at the base of the tower and leads to a substantial aisled nave. (F. W. York)

69 (GKV 69)

Opposite below: Unloading alongside the Coventry Hippodrome in Hales Street is the rather mud-splattered 69 (GKV 69). This Daimler CVA6 with its MCCW H31/29R body has been working on the 5 route from the Coundon area of the city. The bus will subsequently move off to Pool Meadow bus station before returning to suburbia on its outward journey. Following behind it is 30 (FHP 30). Although there are only thirty-nine fleet numbers between them and nominally they are identical, 69 was delivered to the municipal operator some thirteen months after bus 30. (S. N. J. White)

62 (GKV 62)

Above: Parked in Pool Meadow bus station in front of the inspector's office (really little more than a shed!) on 11 June 1963 is 62 (GKV 62). This Daimler CVA6 had the usual Metro-Cammell H31/29R body. The back platform window arrangement was unique to Coventry with twin rear platform windows, with the offside one being tinted black, as was the offside staircase window. The bus, once released from its purdah, will be driven to one of the bus shelters in the left-hand lane in order to pick up its next load of passengers. (W. Ryan)

70 (GKV 70)

Above: Travelling out of the city is 70 (GKV 70), another of the Metro-Cammell-bodied Daimler CVA6s. It is working on an outbound journey to Coundon on the 5A route on 26 August 1961. This route was already in use when it was given the number 5 in June 1928. The bus has just crossed the Coundon Road level crossing alongside the railway station on a line built by the London & North Western Railway in 1850. The level crossing was controlled by a signal box from 1876 until 2009. The road to the right of the railings led to a railway goods yard. (P. Kingston)

77 (GKV 77)

Opposite below: 77 (GKV 77), a Daimler CVA6 with a sixty-seat Metro-Cammell body, is in Hales Street working on a SERVICE EXTRA duty. It has passed the Coventry Theatre and the driver of the bus is about to give a 'turn right' hand signal in order to turn into the entrance to Pool Meadow bus station. 77 has just overtaken a late 1940s Vauxhall Velox LIP six-cylinder saloon dating from the late 1940s. A Bedford CA Utilibrake, registered in Coventry in 1953, travels towards the distant Trinity Street which had by this time been redeveloped in the mid-1950s after its buildings were largely destroyed in the air raid of November 1940. (D. R. Harvey Collection)

71 (GKV 71)

Above: Somewhat poorly parked in Broadgate in the late 1950s, while waiting to leave on the 16A route to Keresley Road, is 71 (GKV 71). This Metro-Cammell-bodied Daimler CVA6 entered service in December 1949. On the far side of Broadgate, behind the speeding Standard Atlas van, is the National Provincial Bank, built in 1930 with a neoclassical portico. The crew sit in the lower saloon as they wait for their departure time to come round on the clock, almost defying any intended passengers to dare to board the bus. At this time, the centre of Broadgate was an attractive grassed open space. At the turn of the twenty-first century this feature would be removed and replaced by a paved open space. (Vectis)

82 (GKV 82)

Above: Travelling into the city centre along Hales Street is Daimler CVA6 82 (GKV 82). The bus is on its way from Copsewood to Broadgate and then across the city to Earlsdon on the 9 route. At this point near to Pool Meadow bus station in Hales Street is the medieval stone-built Swanswell Gate. This was built in about 1440 and was one of twelve gates built into the city wall that led into medieval Coventry. Most of the wall and all but two of the gates were pulled down early into the Restoration period, but Swanswell Gate and Tower Gate survived. Swanswell Gate was even given a pitched roof and converted to a shop. It survived in this form until 1930 when the roof was removed and the castellated battlements were exposed once again. On the right is the original Coventry Central fire station. This was built in 1902 and had soon become a three bay station with three large entrance doors for the fire engines. It was only superseded by the new Radford Road station in 1976; it is now a wine bar and restaurant. Between it and the distant Ford Street is Holy Trinity Church School which was demolished in the 1960s. (A. J. Douglas)

88 (GKV 88)

Opposite below: 88 (GKV 88), a Daimler CVA6 with a Metro-Cammell H31/29R body dating from January 1950, crosses the Coundon Road level crossing on the old 1850-built London & North Western Railway line near to the railway station, which stood to the north-eastern side of the level crossing, to the right of the bus. The bus is on an inbound journey into Pool Meadow bus station when working on the 5 route on Friday 13 March 1959. The Coundon Road railway station was the first station to the east of the main railway station on the Nuneaton line and was very useful for Coventry RFC's ground in the days when they were one of England's elite rugby teams, when they attracted large crowds. (R. F. Mack)

84 (GKV 84)

Above: A new additional bus service was established to Tile Hill South in August 1957 as the 8 route, but it was only after June 1962 that it shared Hales Street with the 20 service to Bedworth. Carrying a slipboard for the Tile Hill South extension is 84 (GKV 84), which on 7 October 1965 is seen turning into the access road to Pool Meadow bus station. Behind it is the second bus to be numbered 205, not the 'White Lady' but a Daimler CVG6 registered SKV 205 dating from January 1957 that is working on the 20 route to Bedworth. (A. J. Douglas)

89 (GKV 89)

Above: The Owen Owen department store dominated the Trinity Street end of the north side of Broadgate and its design, dating from 1954, was typical of the early 1950s architecture that was built in the city centre. Beneath the somewhat fussy upper storey windows is 89 (GKV 89), another of the Metro-Cammell-bodied Daimler CVA6s that constituted one of the largest single order of buses ever delivered to the municipality. The bus is operating along Keresley Road beyond the normal terminus at the Shepherd and Shepherdess public house, on a special service along Tamworth Road to Keresley Hospital that operated four times per day and coincided with the hospital's opening hours. (M. Rooum)

96 (GKV 96)

Opposite below: The very last of the ninety-six Daimler CVA6s arrived from Metro-Cammell in November 1952 as 96 (GKV 96). This chassis had been ordered in February 1946, but Coventry Transport required a new Metro-Cammell body style based on the 1939 EHP-registered batch of Daimler COA6s. The body manufacturer would only build bodies to their selected post-war designs and so, as with 99 (GKV 99), the AEC Regent RT, the 1946 'prototype' body intended for the chassis of 96 was never built and it was eventually bodied as a hybrid exposed radiator bus with both 1948–50 and 1952 design features. The most obvious differences were the 7-inch-deep sliding saloon ventilators, a reduction of two seats in the lower saloon and Lister's moquette upholstery. 96 is loading up with passengers in Broadgate when operating to Earlsdon on the 9 route. Despite the late delivery of the bus it was withdrawn quite early during 1966 and became driver training vehicle 07 for two years. (R. F. Mack)

94 (GKV 94)

Above: 94 (GKV 94) was bought for preservation in 1971 by the 94 Group, having been used for three years from August 1968 by Smiths of Long Itchington. After forty years of intermittent use as a preserved bus, the bodywork was assessed in 2012 and was considered barely worthy of saving due to excessive body pillar corrosion. Under the umbrella of preservationist Roger Burdett, an extensive and expensive restoration scheme has been put in train and 94 might 'hit the road again' by 2017 after a full body rebuild. The bus is here in its first period of restoration in 1973. (A. D. Broughall)

97 (GKV 97)

Above: Daimler's chassis number for 97 (GKV 97) was 12692, which made it numerically the first of all the exposed radiator Daimlers delivered to the Corporation between 1948 and 1952. 97 was the first of two Daimler CVD6s with Metro-Cammell bodies almost identical to those mounted on the CVA6s but fitted with fluorescent lighting. In addition both CVD6s had air brakes. 97 was delivered very late from the bodybuilders in November 1950. It stands in company with Daimler CVA6 91 (GKV 91) and Maudslay Regent III 120 (JKV 120) in Sandy Lane garage yard. (D. R. Harvey Collection)

98 (GKV 98)

Opposite below: The last two of the exposed radiator double-decker buses to be delivered were not the usual Daimler CVA6s but the Daimler CD6 8.6 litre-engined CVD6 model. The last of these pair was 98 (GKV 98), which was eventually delivered in January 1951 and was the only one of the exposed radiator Daimler post-war double-deckers to be equipped with air brakes. The two Daimler CVD6 and the AEC Regent III RT chassis were intended to have prototype bodies built by Metro-Cammell. Pressures to fulfil other large orders meant that one-offs could not be justified and so both 97 and 98 were built with standard Daimler CVA6-style bodies. A traffic inspector walks purposefully towards the immaculate but empty 98 (GKV 98). The bus stands in Pool Meadow bus station when working on the 6 route to Bell Green. (M. A. Sutcliffe)

99 (GKV 99)

Above: Standing in Broadgate on 1 April 1951 is 99 (GKV 99), the AEC Regent III 3RT, which had been in service for only a few weeks. It is operating on the 2 route to Cheylesmore. The chassis was one of the fifty 'provincial' RTs released by AEC in 1946 and 1947, all of which had smaller 900 by 20 sized front tyres which gave the buses a somewhat unbalanced appearance. Unlike all the London RTs, Coventry's 99 was the only one bodied by Metro-Cammell. The Metro-Cammell order for LT was for 450 bodies mounted on Leyland Titan 7RT chassis and this AEC RT chassis was bodied with the 451st body. The thick upper moulding above the middle cream band on the MCCW bodywork was the main external distinguishing feature for the 7RT body. (D. R. Harvey Collection)

99 (GKV 99)

Above: In 1946, fifty of the new AEC Regent RT chassis designed for London Transport were earmarked for the 'provincial' market as the revised AEC Regent III was not ready for production. Their chassis numbers were 0961186–7 and 189–238. LTs two major bodybuilders were Park Royal and Weymann, who worked in unison on this vast project to replace all the remaining tramcar fleet and all the pre-war and wartime buses. The initial progress was slow as jigs had to be made to build the bodies to extremely fine tolerances. Thus with AEC producing large numbers of new RT chassis and no bodies for them, these fifty RT chassis were made available, with five municipalities and four companies taking the completed vehicles between December 1946 and October 1947. One of these post-war RT chassis, 0961217, built in 1946, was intended to have a specially designed Metro-Cammell body but they could only accommodate it as part of the programme to build bodies for RTL-type buses for London Transport and it only entered service in March 1951 after the chassis of what was to become 99 was parked in various locations in the undertakings' various premises for over four years. Almost in despair, the AEC was bodied with an extra London RT type body by MCCW after the completion of 450 London Leyland RTLs, which had all been built at Marston Green. 99 (GKV 99) stands at the outer terminus of the 10 route, Wall Hill Road, Brownshill Green, opposite the White Lion public house. (D. R. Harvey Collection)

99 (GKV 99)

Opposite above: Parked alongside the bus shelter in Eaton Road in May 1959 is 99 (GKV 99). The bus is operating on the 20 route to Longford. 99 had the distinction of being the only AEC Regent III RT type to have a Metro-Cammell RT7 type body and so, by default, Coventry Transport did get its solitary AEC Regent RT with a specially constructed body. The bus was the first one in the fleet to have a sliding cab door, which a few years later would become the norm on MCCW Orion-bodied Daimler CVG6s. Sliding cab doors were ideal when parking buses close together in garages, but it could be a bit of a mountaineering trip for a driver when entering or leaving his cab. (D. F. Parker)

100 (GKV 100)

Above: Parked in Broadgate, just beyond the top of Trinity Street, is Coventry's only Crossley. It was a DD42/7T, with a Brockhouse turbo-transmission gearbox and the latest Crossley HOE7/5 downdraught engine. The chassis number was 94940, which immediately preceded the first of the 260 chassis delivered to Birmingham City Transport, but although the bodywork was very similar to the Crossley bodies supplied to its near neighbour, it was basically another Metro-Cammell Coventry-styled body as per their large order for Daimler CVA6s. The bus is being used on the 22 route to Willenhall and sports the reverse livery previously, and for many years uniquely, carried by 205 (CWK 205), the 1938 Daimler COA6. (A. D. Broughall)

100 (GKV 100)

The unique feature of the Metro-Cammell bodywork on 100 (GKV 100) was the angled bottom to the windscreen. Still fitted with its torque convertor oil header tank on the front bulkhead, this Crossley DD42/7T chassis was first ordered by Coventry Transport in October 1946 yet was not delivered until over four years later. 100 is at the Tile Hill terminus in about 1951 when working on the 8 service. The torque convertor gearbox proved to be unsatisfactory as it reduced the fuel performance of the bus, although the Crossley HOE7/5B proved to be satisfactory. As a result, in 1953 the Crossley HOE7/5B engine was replaced by an AEC 7.7 litre engine with crash gearbox. This engine and transmission combination was later replaced in December 1961 by a fluid flywheel and a preselector gearbox taken from a withdrawn Daimler CWA6. (R. Marshall)

100 (GKV 100)

Known as the 'White Lady', 100 (GKV 100) is working on the 21 route from Lenton's Lane into the city centre to terminate in Broadgate. This solitary Metro-Cammell-bodied Crossley DD42/7T was always painted in the predominantly cream livery and had by this time recently lost its Brockhouse torque convertor and also been re-engined with a standard AEC A173 7.58 litre engine. It is travelling over the traffic lights in Stoney Stanton Road at the junction with Harnall Lane East. The shop with the angled doorway is The Bon Bon confectionery shop, which by 2014 was an optician called The Eye Wear House. The Bon Bon sold Dionisco Di Mascio's ice cream and lollies. Mr Di Mascio came from Cassino in Italy and set up an ice cream factory on King William Street, just off Harnall Lane East in 1932 and continued trading until 1980. D Di's Italian-style ice creams and milk ice lollies were a Coventry speciality. (PM Photography)

101 (GKV 101)

Above: An Austin FX3 taxi travels into Stoney Stanton Road and begins to follow a Coventry Transport bus which is working on the 21 route. 101 (GKV 101) was the undertaking's first new post-war single-decker. The chassis of these vehicles followed on from the later Coventry Daimler CVA6 double-deckers, with 102 along with 101 being delivered in July 1949. The Daimler CVD6 chassis had a very attractive Brush B34F body which was fitted with high-backed dual-purpose type seating and was designed to be used occasionally for private hire work as well as normal service requirements, thus the distinctive predominantly cream reversed livery. The bus is working into the city terminus of the 21 route in Broadgate. (C. W. Routh)

103 (GKV 103)

Opposite above: The route blind has been deliberately wound to half-way between numbers in order to discourage potential passengers getting onto the bus before it was ready to start loading up although, parked as it is, the railings in Broadgate would have been enough of a barrier. From behind 103 (GKV 103), a traffic inspector examines his running lists, though he could not have been too interested in the single-decker as the cab appears to be empty. The earlier buses had the unusually deep Beclawat 12-inch saloon ventilators, which might have been more suited to a bus operating in hotter climes. Unlike the contemporary double-deckers these vehicles had a recessed windscreen in a frame which followed the line between the roof front dome and the cab apron. It is about 1957, as parked behind the distant Daimler CVA6, 37 (GKV 37), working on the 1 route is one of the war-time Guy Arab Is with Manchester-style Weymann bodies that were soon to be taken out of service. One of these attractive buses, 105 (GKV 105), has been the subject of a long ongoing preservation project. (C. W. Routh)

107 (GKV 107)

Above: At Graywood Avenue when working on the 19 route is 107 (GKV 107), one of the well proportioned Brush-bodied Daimler CVD6s. The sixteen chassis were built in two batches and although Brush bodied them in one continuous order the two groups were slightly different with regard to their sliding saloon ventilators, although 110 was the anomaly in that it had the earlier deep sliding ventilators. The split was easy to establish without recourse to finding the chassis numbers as the first half had the last of the GKV registration marks, while the second group had HKV registrations that were first issued in May 1949. These single-deckers were delivered between July and November 1949 and replaced the entire fleet of fifteen pre-war Daimler COG5 single-deckers. (F. W. York)

110 (HKV 110)

Above: Waiting in Pool Meadow bus station to embark on a journey to Berkswell in 1950 is 110 (HKV 110). This was the only one of the later chassis to have the deep saloon ventilators, which made the body look less distinguished. 110, a Brush-bodied Daimler CVD6, is working to Berkswell on the 19 route when barely one year old. This route was acquired from Bunty Motorways four years earlier in April 1936 and remained the only Coventry Transport route to require the use of single-deck vehicles. Standing behind 110 is an as-yet unrebuilt 381 (FDU 381), a Duple-bodied Daimler CWA6D delivered in November 1945. (D. R. Harvey Collection)

108 (GKV 108)

Opposite above: Travelling along Corporation Street is 108 (GKV 108), which was the first of the sixteen Brush-bodied Daimler CVD6 to have shallow saloon ventilators. Delivered in September 1949, this bus was one of seven that were taken out of service in 1963 and was scrapped the following year. The two Daimler CVD6 chassis groups of eight were numbered 14462–9 and were followed by eight more numbered 14689–96. These last eight chassis, according to Daimler records, were intended for Salisbury Municipality in what was then Southern Rhodesia. Salisbury had already received a dozen Daimler CVG5s which all received 30-foot-long Weymann B39F bodywork, so it is possible that the second group of chassis that arrived in Coventry were, nominally at least, a cancelled export order. 108 is being used on a special service 'TO THE FAIRGROUND' whose destination is being displayed on the slipboard mounted on the front bulkhead at the rear of the engine compartment. The single-decker is being overtaken by a 1962 Wolseley 16/60 Farina-styled saloon. (R. H. G. Simpson)

111 (HKV 111)

Above: Fulfilling its secondary role as a vehicle designed for medium distance private hire work is 111 (HKV 111). This Daimler CVD6 had a Brush B34F body layout when new but was one of three to be refitted by S. H. Bond of Wythenshawe in 1954 with coach seats, luggage racks, lighting, heaters and chrome strips fitted along each side and was reclassified as DP30F. Thus it was well suited to a quick run down the A5 before the opening of the M1 in 1958, as in this case to Wembley Stadium. Of the three conversions, 111 was the first to be withdrawn in 1964 whereas 113 and 114 lasted until 1966 and 1967 respectively. (R. H. G. Simpson)

113 (HKV 113)

Above: Black & White coach WDG 634, a 1959 AEC Reliance 2MU3RV with a Roe C41F body, is seen parked alongside Coventry Transport's 113 (HKV 113). This was one of the Daimler CVD6s whose Brush body had been rebuilt with coach seats for medium distance private hire work as late as 1954. Towards the end of the 1950s even this upgrading could not hide the by now rather old-fashioned front-engined layout and they were relegated back to bus operation when, in 1959, three Daimler Freeline G6H/Ss with Willowbrook Viking C41F bodywork were acquired. (R. F. Mack)

117 (JKV 117)

Opposite above: Nine Regent Mark III models were delivered to Coventry Corporation as Maudslays, having been assembled at the company's Castle Maudslay Works in Great Alne near Alcester. As a result they received Maudslay chassis numbers 50001–9 as well as AEC numbers 9612E4639–47. They had Metro-Cammell H31/27R bodywork of that maker's standard sloping-front style for this chassis that was very similar to buses supplied on AEC Regent IIIs for nearby Leicester and Nottingham Corporations, but also built for Dundee and Glasgow Corporations. They all entered service in January 1951 as Coventry's 117–125 and the first one, 117 (JKV 117), is being inspected when first delivered by Mr Fearnley, the General Manager, and members of the Transport Committee. (R. H. G. Simpson)

118 (JKV 118)

Above: The Coventry Regent IIIs were the only post-war Maudslay double-deck chassis to be constructed. Maudslay had been taken over by AEC in 1948 as, along with Crossley Motors, they became part of the ACV group on 1 October of the same year. These buses were built up at the Alcester Works of Maudslay, but although AEC Regent IIIs they were, because of the location of their manufacture, slightly more than badged-up Maudslays. The batch of nine buses for Coventry did at least have the justification of having been assembled in the undertaking's home county. It is reputed that they were supplied to the Corporation to pay off a rates debt, probably owing from the period immediately prior to the merger, when business may not have been buoyant. 118 (JKV 118) is being used on the 17 route to Bagington Village and is at the bus shelters outside the Railway Hotel in Warwick Road. (D. R. Harvey Collection)

121 (JKV 121)

Above: Parked in Eaton Road is 121 (JKV 121), one of the MCCW-bodied Maudslay Regent IIIs. It is working on the 14 Inner Circle route, which was introduced as a new circular service to and from Coventry railway station in both directions in November 1934. 121 is at the bus shelter on May 1956. Eaton Road was named after the Lord of Cheylesmore, who owned the land, was built in 1880 and leads to Coventry railway station, but lost some of its former prestige in the 1960s when the station was rebuilt and the St Patrick's Ringway was constructed as part of Coventry's Inner Ring Road. These buses had four-speed preselector gearboxes coupled to a fluid flywheel and were fitted with air brakes, which perhaps made them less popular than the triple servo vacuum brakes on the CVA6s. (D. F. Parker)

119 (JKV 119)

Opposite above: Basking in the sunshine is 119 (JKV 119). It is parked in Shady Lane near to the bus station in March 1961 before returning on the short journey to return to Sandy Lane Garage. The Maudslay badge is clearly visible at the top of the radiator. These Regent III buses were fitted with standard Metro-Cammell bodies but despite having the large AEC A208 9.6 litre engine, they only seated fifty-eight passengers; the upper saloon seating capacity was the same as the Metro-Cammell-bodywork on the Daimler CVA6s, but the lower saloon was two seats fewer at twenty-seven. All nine of them had quite short lives as they were taken out of service during 1965 and sold for immediate breaking up. (C. Aston)

122 (JKV 122)

Above: Unloading its passengers at the front of the impressive 1902-constructed Coventry Central fire station in Hales Street is 122 (JKV 122). The bus is blocking the entrance to the road between the fire station and Holy Trinity Church School which led into Pool Meadow bus station. Holy Trinity School was a victim of the construction of the Swanswell Ringway around the city centre which, in 1968, was the fifth section to be completed. Just disappearing into the bus station is 60 (GKV 60), a Metro-Cammell-bodied Daimler CVA6. The Maudslay Regent III is operating on the 21 service from Bell Green which terminated in Broadgate. (A. A. Yates)

123 (JKV 123)

Above: Waiting in the middle of Pool Meadow bus station is Maudslay Regent III M9612E 123, (JKV 123). The bus is working on one of Coventry's many works services, in this case to the Armstrong Whitworth Aircraft works at Baginton. These services ran at peak times to take workers to and from the many factories in the city. Most were either car manufacturing companies, such as Humber, Jaguar, Massey Ferguson, Standard and members of the Rootes Group, aircraft manufacturers including Armstrong Whitworth, who also manufactured Armstrong Siddeley luxury cars until 1960, or makers of components and machine tools such as A. C. Wickham and Alfred Herbert. (Vectis)

128 (KVC 128)

Opposite below: Parked at the entrance to Pool Meadow bus station is 128 (KVC 128), a 'New Look' front Daimler CVD6 with an MCCW H31/27R body. It was delivered in January 1952 and was very similar to the equivalent buses delivered to Birmingham City Transport, which by this time had reached fleet number 2757. Behind the bus is the medieval Swanswell Gate, which was built in about 1440 as one of the twelve gates built into the city wall. The bus is displaying the rather anonymous 'SERVICE EXTRA' display and the terminal destination 'CITY POOL MEADOW', which gives little idea of where the bus has either come from or going to! (G. Pattison)

124 (JKV 124)

Above: The as-yet unfinished Leofric Hotel and the buildings on the western side of Broadgate serve as a backdrop to 124 (JKV 124), a then four-year-old Maudslay Regent III 9612E with a Metro-Cammell H31/27R dating from January 1951. Barriers and tape prevent pedestrians gaining access to the still unfinished Precinct. The driver has a quick natter with his conductor before they take their bus on the long journey on the 20 route to Bedworth some 5½ miles away. As a bus route, it replaced the 1 tram service in November 1940 once the decision had been quickly made to abandon the tram system. (D. R. Harvey Collection)

133 (KVC 133)

Above: The Shepherd and Shepherdess was a mock Jacobean half-timbered public house owned by Marston's Brewery. The pub, built in 1936, served as the Keresley Road terminus of the 16 route. It was built behind the old eighteenth-century hostelry but the cellars of the old pub survived and were covered over by the car park, worryingly, just where the bus is standing! The bus is 133 (KVC 133), delivered in January 1952, and was one of the forty Daimler CVD6 vehicles built with Metro-Cammell bodies. This class of bus was the last delivered to Coventry with 'heavyweight' bodies weighing 8 tons 1 cwt. (A. J. Douglas)

131 (KVC 131)

Opposite above: Standing empty outside the Coventry Hippodrome is 131 (KVC 131), a Metro-Cammell-bodied Daimler CVD6 delivered in January 1952 with its Birmingham-style 'New Look' front enhanced by the stylised, chromed, fluted radiator batch. The bus is operating the 7 service to Sewell Highway. These forty buses were the first Daimlers to be delivered to another operator with the Birmingham-style 'New Look' front. After this order was completed, the refined 8.6 litre Daimler CD6 engine became less popular for double-deck chassis and was all but phased out within a couple of years except for a few penny numbers fitted until the end of the decade. (D. R. Harvey Collection)

135 (KVC 135)

Above: 135 (KVC 135), one of the forty fifty-eight-seater Daimler CVD6s with Metro-Cammell bodies, is almost full up as it prepares to leave the bus shelters in Broadgate on the 9 route to Earlsdon in about 1953. The bus is virtually in as-new condition and still retains the full-width, diagonally mounted rear mud flap across the full width of the platform. The bus has an advertisement for Goodwin's Extra Self Raising Flour which adorned many a Coventry Transport bus in the 1950s and 1960s. Goodwin Foster Brown Ltd were based in Dudley and had mills in Hanley, Derby and a large mill in Wheatley Street, Coventry. According to their advertising, Goodwin's 'Extra' Self Raising Flour was 'unequalled for cakes and pastry' and the company produced a series of excellent cookery books, obviously using their flour. (P. Tizard)

137 (KVC 137)

Above: Parked in the turning circle at St James' Lane, Willenhall, is Daimler CVD6 137 (KVC 137). The conductress takes the weight off her feet as she sits on the long nearside seat in the lower saloon while the driver sits in his cab waiting for the bell to go. 137 is working on the 22 route, which had been extended to Willenhall in July 1956. The bus is turning right onto London Road on its way back towards the city centre. Behind the bus is Willenhall's post office while on the right is J. Gilmartin's shop, which has a pair of advertisements for Tizer, (The Appetizer), which is a citrus-flavoured fizzy drink. To the left of the bus is a Hillman Minx Series I dating from about 1957. (R. Marshall)

138 (KVC 138)

Opposite above: The Leofric Hotel was opened on 28 April 1955 by the Lord Mayor of Coventry, having cost £800,000 to build. This was an important building in the City Architect Donald Gibson's vision of Broadgate. Located on the west side of Broadgate and adjacent to the trailblazing Upper Precinct pedestrianised shopping area, the Leofric Hotel had 120 bedrooms as well as a restaurant and the Black Eagle bar, the latter quickly becoming one of the most popular 'watering holes' in Coventry's city centre. The plaque on the wall of the hotel is the very same Black Eagle which was the motif for the hotel. The bus parked outside the hotel in Broadgate is 138 (KVC 138), one of the attractive Metro-Cammell-bodied Daimler CVD6s of 1952, which is working on the 21 to Bell Green. Parked behind the bus is a Birmingham-registered 1953 Austin A70 Hereford saloon. (M. Hayhoe)

145 (KVC 145)

Above: Turning out of Broadgate and into Trinity Street in front of the post-war Owen Owen department store is 145 (KVC 145). This Daimler CVD6 with a MCCW H31/27R body is being followed by a Coventry-registered Triumph Herald of 1960 and an Austin A40 Farina Mk II, suggesting that the lack of advertising on the double-decker is not because it is new but rather that it has just been repainted at the Sandy Lane Works. The Birmingham 'New Look' concealed radiators on these buses were the first to be fitted to any Daimlers built for orders other than for BCT. Daimler fitted this order for Coventry with a stylised fluted Daimler radiator decoration which became their normal standard decorative feature on all subsequent half-cab double-deckers. The bus is operating on the 16 service to Keresley, but on this particular journey, judging by the distribution of the passengers, a single-decker would have been more appropriate. (H. W. Peers)

148 (KVC 148)

Above: The immaculately presented 148 (KVC 148) is parked at the east end of Pool Meadow bus station. It is full up with passengers who await the driver and conductor to take them to Walsgrave. The bus, a Metro-Cammell Birmingham-style bodied Daimler CVD6, is virtually new and would give its passengers a very comfortable ride with its smooth Daimler 8.6-litre engine. The only problem with this engine was that the timing chain was at the back of the engine, which meant that the engine had to be removed in order to change it, and in later life the CD6 unit tended to consume more engine oil than an equivalent Gardner-engined bus. (F. W. York)

152 (KVC 152)

Opposite below: The KVC-registered Daimler CVD6s reveals just how close the Metro-Cammell bodywork was to the 2031–2130 batch of buses supplied to Birmingham City Transport and also how the specification was altered to meet with the requirements of Mr Ronald Fearnley, the General Manager. Two distinguishing features on the 'New Look' front were that the radiator filler cap was mounted externally on the top of the cowling and that in the flying badge just below the bonnet handle was a letter D rather than the letters BCT for those buses delivered to Birmingham City Transport. 152 (KVC 152) is passing the medieval Swanswell Gate in Hales Street with White Street in the distance on 7 October 1965 while working into the city on the 9A route from the Devonshire Arms terminus on Sewall Highway. This was an extension of the Copsewood service, which was introduced in 1964 as a peak-hour extension. (A. J. Douglas)

156 (KVC 156)

Above: Unlike many operators of buses with BCT 'New Look' style concealed radiators, the Coventry buses always retained the full-length front wings. Elsewhere in the country many operators cut the wings back by anything up to a foot in order to improve the flow of air onto the front brakes which, while effective in that respect, did little for the aesthetic appearance of the buses. The conductor of 156 (KVC 156) leans against the railings in front of the snack bar in the temporary shops in Broadgate that lasted for twenty years. The bus is loading up with passengers in the shadow of the largely fourteenth-century Perpendicular Gothic-styled Holy Trinity parish church which towers over the city centre. Behind 156 are two of the later Daimler CVG6s with MCCW Orion bodywork; working on the 20 service is 249 (VWK 249), dating from August 1958, and in the distance with the white roof is 307 (307 RW), which entered service in August 1961. (R. Wellings)

158 (KVC 158)

Above: Parked in the outer reaches of Pool Meadow bus station is 158 (KVC 158), another of the 1952 New Look front Daimler CVD6s. The Metro-Cammell bodies were the last 'Birmingham lookalike' vehicles to be built. This type of body was first introduced in July 1947 and the last of these CVD6s for Coventry were finally delivered in October 1952. These bodies were some of the last MCCW products to have the lower and upper saloons constructed separately. The continual glazing on the off side of the lower saloon gave a somewhat single-deck looking body, caused by the need for the half-turn staircase not to intrude into the lower saloon while allowing a certain amount of natural light to illuminate the stairwell. 158 was finally withdrawn in November 1971. (S. N. J. White)

161 (KVC 161)

Opposite below: The bus stop in Broadgate for the 16 service to Keresley was in the angle of the square, with the Leofric Hotel behind the bus while in front of it is the Owen Owen department store. This frequently resulted in buses having to park very awkwardly with the intending passengers having to take several paces into the road in order to reach their vehicle. Here 161 (KVC 161), a 1952-vintage, Metro-Cammell-bodied Daimler CVD6 shows the problem, resolved in later years by deliveries of front-entrance, rear-engined buses such as the Daimler Fleetline and Leyland Atlantean. (Vectis)

159 (KVC 159)

Above: Waiting at the bus stop at Mount Street in Allesley Old Road is bus 159 (KVC 159). The Daimler CVD6 has a Metro-Cammell H31/27R body and is working on the 10 route from Brownshill Green on 3 July 1960 as it travels towards the city terminus in Pool Meadow bus station. The bus is at the point where the distant late-Victorian villas gave way to interwar semi-detached houses which were separated from the main carriageway by a service road. It has come from the junction with Holyhead Road, which in the nineteenth century had a toll house where it joined Allesley Old Road on the Thomas Telford-designed road to London. (R. F. Mack)

162 (KVC 162)

Leaving Pool Meadow bus station on Friday 17 March 1967 is 162 (KVC 162). This rather tired-looking Metro-Cammell-bodied Daimler CVD6 has been working from Tile Hill Lane at the junction with Banner Lane on an 8 route service. To the left are the Midland Red bus shelters, which were always divided off from the Corporation side of the bus station. Parked at Midland Red's Stand 4 is a seventy-two-seater BMMO D9 being used on the busy 159 route back to Birmingham via Meriden and Stonebridge. By this time the old pre-war vintage bus station was beginning to look a little time expired but it took many years before the new Pool Meadow was opened in 1993. (Photofives)

165 (KVC 165)

Travelling along Hales Street as it approaches Pool Meadow bus station is the last of the forty Daimler CVD6s. 165 (KVC 165), along with the preceding vehicle, was very late to enter service, having only been delivered from the bodybuilder in October 1952, some three months after 163 had arrived. One of the 1965 Bedford VAS1s with Marshall B30F bodywork makes its way out of Ford Street from the bus station and into Hales Street. This road and all the adjoining properties were soon to be swept away when Coventry's ring road was built. Following on behind 165 is a 1958 Daimler CVG6. This is 246 (VWK 246), which was one of forty buses delivered in 1958, but for the first time with the 'Manchester' concealed radiator. (D. R. Harvey Collection)

The Lightweight Era

3132 (MOF 132)

If the Metro-Cammell Orion lightweight body on REH 500 would lead the way to future body orders, the five-cylinder CLG5 chassis was a step too far. The Daimler CD6 engine was already being phased out and with Coventry Transport more or less obliged to support local industry, the Daimler CVG6 was the only real alternative bus chassis. The problem was that Coventry had never operated a bus equipped with a Gardner 6LW 8.4 litre engine. As another trial, Birmingham City Transport 3132 (MOF 132), with a Crossley H30/25R body that had been new in time for the final Erdington group of tramway abandonment on 4 July 1953, was used with its Birmingham municipal crests removed as a demonstrator by Transport Holdings (Daimler), Coventry, to Coventry Corporation from 15 December 1953 until 28 December 1953. The following month it fulfilled the same purpose with Glasgow Corporation. On its last day of demonstration in Coventry, MOF 132 turns out of the still incomplete Broadgate when working on the 21 service to Alderman's Green. The trial with this bus was successful and led to a total of 171 of the CVG6 chassis being ordered by Coventry Transport. (T. J. Edgington)

REH 500

During 1953 Coventry Transport tried out three buses for demonstration purposes. The bus that 'won' the body building contract was REH 500. Originally intended to be a Daimler CVD6, the chassis was rebuilt to a lightweight specification and as chassis number 18334 became the first of only two CLG5s to be constructed, having a five-cylinder Gardner 5LW 7.0-litre engine. The chassis was delivered to the bodybuilders on 31 August 1952 and became the sensation of the 1952 Commercial Motor Show when it was displayed on Metro-Cammell's stand at Earl's Court as Potteries Motor Tractions 500 with the distinctive registration of REH 500. The bus had the new lightweight Orion body with a H32/26R body layout and was the only one to have equal-depth saloon windows; it was, however, extremely spartan. The whole bus weighed only 6 tons 2cwt, but the body only contributed 36¼ cwt to this total. Prior to its acceptance by PMT, in February 1953, REH 500 was demonstrated to Coventry Transport in its full PMT all-over red livery and is parked in Trinity Street, just beyond the medieval buildings in Priory Row. (D. R. Harvey Collection)

RWK

Above: One of the RWK-registered batch of twenty-five Daimler CVG6s is posed by Metro-Cammell in 1956 with its skeletal bodywork exposed in order to show the method of construction. All of the framework is complete and the stress panels in the lower saloon and in the front and rear pair of bays in the upper saloon are in place. The main roof structure has been attached to the upper saloon body pillars but the fibre-glass front and rear domes have yet to be inserted. (D. R. Harvey Collection)

7194 H

Opposite above: On loan to Glasgow Corporation in the same condition that it was demonstrated to Coventry Transport is the experimental 7194 H. A lightened but basically completely conventional version of the reduced-weight AEC Regent III in 7.58-litre form was introduced as the 6813S, with new synchromesh gearbox. It was bodied in 1953 as a fifty-eight-seater by Park Royal as a prototype using aluminium alloy frames. This resulted in the complete vehicle weighing only 6 tons 12 cwt, and the RT-style bodywork looked most handsome in the livery of City of Oxford Motor Services. In a lot of respects, this was AEC's re-development chassis for later plans, which in 1954 was introduced as the new the Regent V model. Coventry Transport was never going to be tempted to purchase such a vehicle from the ACV Group but it did show how economic strictures were beginning to exert an influence on the future ordering policy of municipalities such as Coventry. (D. R. Harvey Collection)

168 (RWK 168)

Above: Leaving Harnall Lane Garage is 168 (RWK 168), which had entered service in January 1956. It is being used as a driver training vehicle and the instructor can be seen leaning through the front bulkhead cab window. At least the trainee didn't have to struggle with a crash gearbox any longer when learning to drive, as from about 1960 onwards all the Coventry bus fleet were equipped with preselector gearboxes. 168 was the third bus in the 1955 order for twenty-five buses which introduced the Gardner 6LW engine and the lightweight MCCW Orion body into the fleet for the first time as the combined product of the demonstration visits of REH 500, with its prototype Orion bodywork, and the Daimler CVG6 MOF 132, equipped with the 8.4 litre Gardner engine. (D. Williams)

170 (RWK 170)

Above: A sample of post-war Coventry Transport buses, all with Metro-Cammell bodywork, leaves Pool Meadow Bus Station. The trio is led by 92 (GKV 92), a 1950 Daimler CVA6, while at the rear is 256 (VWK 256), a Daimler CVG6 with the later 'Manchester' type of concealed radiator cowl. The middle vehicle working on the 8A route to Tile Hill is 170 (RWK 170), a Daimler CVG6 that had entered service in January 1956 and was fitted with a Birmingham 'New Look' concealed radiator distinguished by the large fluted and chromed 'eyebrow' Daimler motif. 170 was one of the first of the class to be withdrawn in 1971. (R. H. G. Simpson)

173 (RWK 173)

Opposite below: The RWK-registered buses were the first ones in the fleet to have sliding cab doors. These were a mixed blessing; the sliding door certainly allowed buses to be parked closer together in the garage but the higher lip to the bottom of the cab meant that the driver had to haul himself over the bottom of the entrance and then down into the cab, whose floor was very nearly 2 feet below the entrance. The second problem was that the door could either slide open or closed under acceleration or deceleration. 173 (RWK 173) stands with only the conductress on board in Hales Street outside the Coventry Theatre, which until 1955 was the Coventry Hippodrome. The bus is working on the 18 service from Canley. (G. Pattison)

171 (RWK 171)

Above: Although the lightweight bodywork was fairly basic, the Coventry specification required comfortable seating, with that in the lower saloon covered with moquette and the upper saloon with leathercloth. The buses were 8 feet wide and had a white steering wheel to remind the driver that the buses were 6 inches wider. They were also 27 feet long, making them a foot longer than the KVC-registered buses. 171 (RWK 171), a sixty-seater Metro-Cammell-bodied Daimler CVG6, is parked in Eaton Road near to Coventry railway station and is about to depart for the long run to Bedworth via Broadgate on the 20 route. (R. H. G. Simpson)

175 (RWK 175)

Above: Turning from Bishop Street into Hales Street when working into the city centre and then on to the railway station from Bedworth on the 20 route is 175 (RWK 175). It is alongside the old Free Grammar School, which used these medieval premises from 1557 until 1885 but which was built in the second quarter of the fourteenth century in red sandstone as the chapel to the former Hospital of St John. The bus is a still fairly new Daimler CVG6 with a Metro-Cammell H33/27R body as it was delivered for service in February 1956. Behind the bus are a 1954 Sheffield-registered Ford Consul EOTA and a Morris Minor delivery van. (D. R. Harvey Collection)

180 (RWK 180)

Opposite below: Once the debris from the wartime air raids had been cleared, the top end of Trinity Street and beyond into Broadgate remained largely unaltered as the redevelopment on the western side of Broadgate and The Precinct continued apace. The immediately post-war 'temporary' shops in front of Holy Trinity parish church, just beyond the front of bus 180 (RWK 180), were built in 1947 on the eastern side of Broadgate, lasting until 1974. The almost new Metro-Cammell-bodied Daimler CVG6 is waiting to resume its journey to Willenhall on the 22 route, having arrived in the city centre from Sewall Highway, a route which had been introduced in January 1955. Behind the bus are the medieval buildings in Priory Row while dominating the skyline is the timber-framed building which, with its jettied frontage and large bay windows, looked medieval but was actually built in 1938. (A. J. Owen)

180 (RWK 180)

Above: Later in its life, 180 (RWK 180) waits at the bus shelters in Pool Meadow bus station in April 1967 when working on the 4 route to Wyken. The livery is the same as before save for the small script COVENTRY TRANSPORT name. The bus has got an advertisement for Permoglaze paints, whose origins date back to a Manchester-based company set up in 1884. 180 was delivered to Coventry Transport in December 1955 and was withdrawn in 1972, being replaced by a batch of East Lancashire-bodied Daimler Fleetlines. Parked in the distance, near to the entrance to the bus station, is one of the three 1967 Bristol RESL6Gs with dual-doorway ECW bodies. (M. S. Gunn)

183 (RWK 183)

Above: A BMW Isetta three-wheeler bubble car with a 295cc engine speeds in the opposite direction, past the oncoming Corporation bus. 183 (RWK 183) is working on the 18 route to Canley crematorium, a service introduced during March 1955 which crossed the A45 Fletchamstead Highway. This Daimler CVG6 had the usual lightweight all-metal framed MCCW Orion H33/27R body, entered service in December 1955 and remained in service for just over fifteen years. The Birmingham-style 'New Look' concealed radiator was fitted mainly to Daimlers and Guy Arab IVs, but was also built on some late examples of AEC Regent IIIs and famously on Birmingham's last 100 Crossley DD42/6s, delivered in 1950. There was a mixed response to the design, but its slightly bulbous shape did somewhat mask the utilitarian appearance of the Orion bodywork. (D. R. Harvey Collection)

189 (RWK 189)

Opposite below: Climbing up the steep rise in Trinity Street from Hales Street soon after it was made a one-way street in the mid-1960s is 189 (RWK 189). This Daimler CVG6 had a MCCW H33/27R body and was the penultimate member of the twenty-five buses ordered in 1955. The bus is operating on the 20 route from Bedworth. The only car in sight is a late 1962 Coventry-registered Wolseley Hornet I. This was a slightly more upmarket version of an Austin Mini but with a vertical Wolseley radiator with an illuminated badge, a bustle boot, tailfins and a wood veneer-covered dashboard, although it still had sliding door windows which were replaced by more normal wind-up windows when the Hornet II was introduced in 1963. (D. R. Harvey Collection)

187 (RWK 187)

Above: Standing in Broadgate in 1963, outside the Owen Owen department store completed in 1954, is another of the 1955 order of RWK-registered Daimler CVG6s with Metro-Cammell bodies. 187 (RWK 187) is being used on the 16A service to Keresley Road when it was halfway through its operational life. The bus would have been due, or had just received, its seven-year Certificate of Fitness Test. The common practice was that this first test would also be for between five and seven years after which, in the case of many operators, the bus would be taken out of service. In the case of 187 this bus was taken out of use in 1972, thus achieving sixteen years of service. (R. Wellings)

190 (RWK 190)

Opposite: 190 (RWK 190) stands in Broadgate when working on the 21 route to Alderman's Green. This bus was the last of the RWK batch of Daimler CVG6s with MCCW Orion bodies. The rear of these buses was very workmanlike with a large platform window and a deep cutaway on the rear corner to ensure that if the bus was unfortunate enough to turn over, this aperture would serve as an emergency exit. The minimum width for this was about 18 inches, but on the Orion body it was more, which resulted in the nearside rear lights having to be mounted on an extension at the bottom of the rear panel in order to conform to the 1956 Construction and Use Regulations. This also allowed for the operation of 30-foot-long double-deckers on two axles for the first time. 190 was one of two buses whose seating capacity was experimentally increased in 1960 by three seats, having a H34/29R seating layout. (R. Wilson)

191 (SKV 191)

Above: Passing through Broadgate on its way to Coventry railway station when working on the 20 route is 191 (SKV191). This was the first of the 1956 batch of Daimler CVG6s with Metro-Cammell Orion H33/27R bodywork and it arrived in November of that year. These buses were virtually the same as the RWK-registered vehicles and had the same style of Birmingham 'New Look' concealed radiator. Behind the bus is the large replacement Owen Owen department store which from the mid-1950s was the shop in Coventry city centre. The destination winding handle is parallel to the nearside of the driver's cab. (R. F. Mack)

193 (SKV 193)

Above: 193 (SKV 193) stands in Eaton Road, near to the railway station. This MCCW-bodied Daimler CVG6 is working on the 20 route across the city centre to Bedworth that replaced the 1 tram route when the tram system was forced to be abandoned after the 14 November 1940 bombing raid. 193 looks as though it is in need of a repaint as where the advertisement was located between the decks on the offside is far shinier and less weathered than the rather drab maroon elsewhere on the bus. It looks as though it has been hard work for the driver as he is down to his shirt sleeves. (R. H. G. Simpson)

197 (SKV 197)

Opposite above: Climbing up the steep hill in Bishop Street from the distant Burges is Daimler CVG6 197 (SKV 197). This bus is working on the 2 route to Radford and is passing the Castle Hotel on the corner of King Street. Parked opposite the pub is a two-tone, six-cylinder Vauxhall Cresta PA. The Castle Inn was an eighteenth-century building with an impressive frontage on Bishop Street and stood approximately on the site of Bishop Gate on the main entrance to the city from the north. The pub became the Castle Hotel in the mid-twentieth century. By the time bus 197 went passed the Castle on 13 March 1959 it was in terminal decline. It was demolished in the 1960s as part of the 'redevelopment' for the building of the Ring Road. (F. W. York)

198 (SKV 198)

Opposite below: Daimler CVG6 198 (SKV 198) waits at the Tile Hill terminus of the 8 route in 1961. The crew are sitting in the lower saloon and, as if to emphasise the point that they were on their break, the sliding cab door is firmly shut. The rudimentary shelters used by intending passengers offered little protection during inclement weather and it would be many years before bus shelters would offer the waiting passengers some protection. The chassis of 198 had the narrow-width front track of the CVG6 chassis, giving the impression that the 8-foot-wide Metro-Cammell body was somehow perched over the front axle. This bus would end its days being used by Smith of Long Itchington in its contract and school service bus fleet. (D. R. Harvey Collection)

203 (SKV 203)

Above: Although it always looked as if it was ready to be replaced, the old Pool Meadow bus station served the city very well. It had simple but fairly element-proof bus shelters and had reasonably good access for passengers and buses alike. Buses arrived, unloaded and their crews usually left the bus; certainly the cabs of the buses were invariably empty until just before the allotted departure time. 203 (SKV 203) stands in the bus station prior to taking up its next journey to Tile Hill Village on the 8 route. On the wall of the bus station is an advertisement for Benson & Hedges Sterling cigarettes, which had been introduced in the 1960s and was intended to be an upmarket brand. The bus, on the other hand, is advertising Mitchells & Butler's Sam Brown bottled brown ale, known for its sweet, nutty flavour, which was brewed at Cape Hill in Smethwick. (M. S. Gunn)

200 (SKV 200)

Opposite above: Travelling away from Hales Street, Daimler CVG6 200 (SKV 200) accelerates up the hill in Trinity Street when working into the city centre terminus at Broadgate on the 22 service from Willenhall on 24 June 1969. Despite its somewhat down-at-heel look, 200 had another three and a half years of service in front of it. It is being overtaken by a 1966 rear-engine Singer Chamois which was an upmarket version of the Hillman Imp. The buildings on the left were built in 1937 when Trinity Street was completed while the gaunt frontage of the Coventry Hippodrome is visible on the skyline. (A. J. Douglas)

206 (SKV 206)

Above: Turning into Hales Street from Ford Street as it leaves Pool Meadow bus station is 206 (SKV 206), a Daimler CVG6s with a Metro-Cammell H33/27R body. Ford Street and all the adjoining properties were soon to be swept away when Coventry's ring road was built. It is Saturday 26 August 1961 and 206 is working on the 8A route to Tile Hill North in the western suburbs of the city. 206 entered service in January 1957, at the same time that the 8A route had been introduced. This new service branched off Tile Hill Lane and went northwards along Bushbery Avenue, Tile Hill, to a new terminus in Jardine Crescent. (D. R. Harvey Collection)

209 (SKV 209)

Above: On a rainy day 209 (SKV 209) turns from Park Road into Manor Road as it leaves the area near to the railway station when operating on the 20 route to Bedworth by way of Broadgate. This part of Coventry, with its tree-lined roads and large late-Victorian villas, belied its location close to the railway station. The bus is one of the twenty-five SKV-registered Daimler CVG6s with H33/27R lightweight bodywork by Metro-Cammell which, with a weight of 7 tons 1 cwt, was exactly one ton lighter than the previous KVC series Daimler CVD6s. (F. W. York)

214 (SKV 214)

Opposite below: 214 (SKV 214) turns in front of the Coventry Hippodrome in Hales Street. The Daimler CVG6, which had a Metro-Cammell body, is operating on the 21 service to Bell Green. The sliding cab door is firmly closed as, legally at least, buses with these doors should run with them shut, but realistically it was very tempting to drive the bus with the door open. Appearing in the spring of 1963 at the theatre were Cliff Richard and The Shadows, who were embarking on tours with other popular singers of the day around old variety theatres rather than continue with their early career as a rock n' roll stars. (Vectis)

211 (SKV 211)

Above: 211 (SKV 211) passes into Broadgate when being operated by Sandy Lane garage on the 21 service. 211 was the only Coventry Transport bus to be transferred as an operating PSV to West Midlands PTE on 1 April 1974 that had a Birmingham-style 'New Look' concealed radiator. It was renumbered 211Y and was one of twenty-three Daimler CVG6s to be transferred to Acocks Green garage in July to replace a similar number of BCT Standard Daimler CVG6s and Guy Arab IIIs which were due for withdrawal. The bus was immediately renumbered 1211 as the Y suffix on the fleet number could be mistaken for a '7', soon repainted in the PTE Oxford Blue and cream livery and put to work on the Outer Circle route, where it ran until the end of half-cab bus operation in Birmingham on 31 October 1977. (A. D. Broughall)

215 (SKV 215)

Opposite: The last of the SKV-registered Daimler CVG6s was delivered in March 1957 with a standard Birmingham-style 'New Look' concealed radiator coupled to the normal MCCW Orion body. After a few weeks in service, 215 (SKV 215) was withdrawn and sent back to Daimler for a prototype 'Manchester' front to be fitted. This had been developed in collaboration with Manchester Corporation and was intended to improve nearside visibility from the driver's cab. As a result, the bonnet lid was thin and tapered and the whole assembly had a narrow, rather plain glass-fibre front bonnet with a coarsely slatted grill. The offside headlight was in the cab apron and the nearside one located in the mudguard. 215 was the first Daimler CVG6 to operate with the Manchester front (or should the generic name be the Coventry front?). 215 could always be easily identified firstly by the gap in the cab apron and below the windscreen as the new narrow concealed radiator did not fit cleanly into the space vacated by the original 'New Look' front. Secondly, 215 had a smaller Daimler scroll than all subsequent deliveries. The bus is turning from Broadgate into Ironmonger Row when working on the 20 route to Longford. (L. Mason)

SDU 711

Above: On loan during October 1956 was Daimler demonstrator SDU 711. This was a Daimler CVG6 with Willowbrook H37/29RD bodywork which had first entered service during January 1956. This bus had several features that Daimler was trying out with a view to producing a wider range of options on their CVG models. SDU 711 had a Twiflex coupling that was being evaluated against the standard fluid flywheel. By eliminating the usual body underframe, the body was built as low as possible while retaining a centre upper saloon gangway. The low waistline was a revealing feature of this body design, fifteen of which were also supplied to Walsall Corporation. SDU 711 is in Milton Street, Nottingham, in July 1956 when operating on the 57 route. (G. H. F. Atkins)

VKV 99

Above: The second 30-foot-long Daimler CVG6/30 to be built was VKV 99. This chassis had a Gardner 6LW 8.4-litre engine and was bodied by Willowbrook with a H41/33R seating layout. The bus is standing in the demonstration park at the 1956 Commercial Motor Show at Earls Court. This large bus was on hire to Coventry from Daimler during 1957 but although mechanically the same as the shorter CVG6s still being ordered by Mr Fearnley, this bus was considered to be 'three foot too far'. The result was that this type of bus was never operated by Coventry Transport, though some seven years later the large seating capacity was normal for the future rear-engined bus fleet. (A. Richardson)

216 (VWK 216)

Opposite below: Standing in front of the former Midland Red garage in Upper Holland Street on 4 September 1975 is 216 (VWK 216). This was the first of the fifty Daimler CVG6s delivered from new with the 'Manchester' front. The bus entered service in June 1958 and was one of forty to be taken over by WMPTE on 1 April 1974. This bus had been withdrawn in late 1973 but had been reinstated for work elsewhere in the West Midlands operating area in June 1974. Here it could replace 'less fortunate' elderly buses when it was realised that, although redundant in Coventry due to the arrival of new East Lancs-bodied Daimler Fleetlines, these CVG6 had a few more years that could be rung out of them. Still in Coventry's Marshall Red and Shetland ivory livery that had been introduced, the bus has WM fleetnames and has been renumbered 1216. It would remain in service until the spring of 1976. (E. V. Trigg)

217 (VWK 217)

Above: 217 (VWK 217) was one of four of the VWK-registered 1958 batch of Metro-Cammell-bodied Daimler CVG6s to be delivered with a cream-painted roof which served as the trial vehicles for the 291–312 class of 1961. This bus entered service in June 1958 and is being used on the 20 route when virtually new and is preparing to go on the short section of the route from Broadgate to Coventry railway station. 220 is standing at the top of Trinity Street. In the mid-1930s the run-down buildings in Great Butcher Row and the Bull Ring were demolished to make way for Trinity Street. At the top of this new road a large steel-framed building was built in 1938. This huge mock Tudor building was originally called Priory Gate. This building had an applied timber frame, jetties, bay windows, balconies, gables and tall brick chimneys and was joined to the genuinely medieval Lych Gate Cottages located in Priory Row behind the bus on the right. (D. R. Harvey Collection)

220 (VWK 220)

Above: 220 (VWK220), a former Coventry Transport Daimler CVG6 with a Metro-Cammell Orion H33/27R body, has been renumbered 1220 and been repainted in WMPTE livery, which totally alters its appearance. It is travelling away from the centre of Harborne, Birmingham, along Lordswood Road, going towards Hagley Road at Bearwood on the 11C route. By this time the transferred Coventry Daimlers were allocated to Acocks Green garage. It is passing on its nearside Harborne Swimming Baths, which were originally opened on 13 December 1923, next to a house that was occupied for a time by the poet W. H. Auden. The baths were rebuilt at a cost of £12 million and reopened on 3 January 2012. The distant WMPTE Daimler Fleetline is passing the not so lucky Duke of York public house, which was demolished and replaced by a complex of flats around 2001. (D. R. Harvey)

221 (VWK 221)

Opposite above: Daimler CVG6 221 (VWK 221) was another of the quartet of buses delivered in 1958 that was painted with an all-over white roof, giving the bus a more 'cheerful' appearance. It is not long after the new one-way system was introduced in June 1962, when the inbound 15 route to Whitmore Park was diverted from The Burges and ran instead along Hales Street and Trinity Street in order to reach its terminus in Broadgate. 221 had the unusual distinction of not being sold to a dealer after it was withdrawn, as on becoming the first of the class to be taken out of service in 1970 it was broken up by the Corporation themselves for spares at Sandy Lane. (F. W. York)

224 (VWK 224)

Above: The 9 route to Earlsdon left Broadgate via Hertford Street in order to gain Warwick Road and Ratcliffe Road. This meant passing beneath the 1950s bridge which was part of the redevelopment plan for the city centre. On the opposite side of Broadgate, Owen Owen's department store is having one of its frequent sales while a booted Standard Vanguard Phase II circles the open space with Lady Godiva's statue at the centre of Broadgate. 224 (VWK 224), a 1958 Metro-Cammell-bodied Daimler CVG6, enters Hertford Street being followed by a Ford Popular 100E car, one of the last to have the old 1,172cc side valve engine. The VWK-registered buses and subsequent CVG6s were fitted with cab and interior heaters, increasing the weight of these buses to 7 tons 6 cwt. (R. F. Mack)

229 (VWK 229)

Above: The crew of 229 (VWK 229) sit on the kerb edge before heading to Stoke Aldermoor. In the distance is Foleshill Gas Works, which was constructed in 1909. Surviving until the 1970s, the importance of the gasworks began to decline and the gasometers were demolished in 2002 and the site was redeveloped into the Arena Retail Park and Ricoh Arena. The bus is a Daimler CVG6 with a Metro-Cammell Orion body and is parked at the terminus of the 3 route off Holbrook Lane in the north of the city. Parked on the waste ground is a wartime Bedford OW lorry fitted with a 5-ton flatbed vehicle and the sloping, plain military-style bonnet. (R. F. Mack)

233 (VWK 233)

Opposite below: In their declining years, twenty-three of the Metro-Cammell-bodied Daimler CVG6s were repainted in WM PTE blue and cream and had their fleet numbers increased by 1,000. 1233 (VWK 233), allocated to Acocks Green garage, is climbing the hill in Bromford Lane, Erdington, just beyond The Lad In The Lane public house, previously known as The Green Man, a building which dates back to exactly 1400. 1233 is working on the 11A route in July 1977. The cream-painted bulkhead behind the bonnet revealed that the bus was repainted at Tyburn Road Works. (D. R. Harvey)

237 (VWK 237)

Above: On 10 April 1962, 237 (VWK 237) is parked at the Allesley bus shelter in Pool Meadow bus station when working on the 23 route. Unusually, the driver is sitting in his cab and has been there long enough to enjoy reading his newspaper. Behind the bus is 217 (VWK 217), one of the four VWK-registered buses to have been delivered with a cream roof. Despite this livery modification both buses are the standard Coventry Transport fayre of the period, being Daimler CVG6s with Metro-Cammell Orion H33/27R bodywork, with 237 having been delivered to the undertaking in July 1958 and 217 during the previous month. (S. N. J. White)

238 (VWK 238)

Above: The destination boxes for Coventry buses were never big enough to carry more than the basic information and so the solution was found in adopting the 'wedge' lettering. 238 (VWK 238) shows this type of presentation on both the nearside and side destination boxes with the display of Glendower Avenue. On 3 September 1959, this Daimler CVG6 had recently left its terminus outside the Council House in High Street and, having negotiated Broadgate, is about to turn into Ironmonger Row before descending The Burges and turning left into Corporation Street before heading out to the terminus beyond Whoberley Avenue. This service had been introduced in March 1932. VWK 238 sports an advertisement for Flowers Keg Bitter which was brewed in Stratford-upon-Avon. It had been introduced in the late 1950s and at this time cost about a shilling a pint! Travelling towards Broadgate in front of the steps on the left which led to Prior Row is a 1937 Lanchester Eleven saloon car. On the right is 328 (EKV 828), a 1943 Weymann-bodied Guy Arab II which is working out its last weeks of service and would be withdrawn later in 1959. (A. J. Douglas)

239 (VWK 239)

Opposite above: Two of the four preserved Daimler CVG6s with Metro-Cammell Orion bodies are parked next to each other at the erstwhile Aston Manor Transport Museum at Witton, Birmingham, on 9 July 2006. 239 (VWK 239) is owned by the Travel de Courcey Bus Company and 334 (334 CRW) is preserved by the Aston Manor Transport Museum. The former vehicle dates from July 1958 and the latter from November 1963, with 334 seating sixty-three passengers, just three more than the earlier bus. This later bus had a fluid friction clutch with pre-selector gearbox instead of a Wilson pre-selector gearbox. (D. R. Harvey)

246 (VWK 246)

Above: Parked at its terminus outside the Coventry Theatre in Hales Street is 246 (VWK 264). This 1958 Daimler CVG6 is waiting to depart on the 7 route to Sewall Highway. The bus has a Manchester-style concealed radiator, unlike 173 (RWK 173) behind it, which has a Birmingham 'New Look' front, working on the 18 service to Canley. The two Coventry buses both had Metro-Cammell H33/27R bodies, but their different fronts gave the vehicles a very different appearance. Passing away toward Corporation Street is a Midland Red Leyland-bodied LD8 class Leyland Titan PD2/12. (G. Pattison)

249 (VWK 249)

Above: In early West Midlands PTE days in late 1974, 249 (VWK 249) turns from the top of Trinity Street into the short remnant of Ironmonger Row and then down the steep hill in The Burges. This Harnall Lane Daimler CVG6 is working to Wood End, but already standards have slightly slipped as the bus, which should be showing the number 21, apparently has not got a front destination number blind. The bus has been renumbered 249Y, signifying that it worked its last few years in Coventry, which had become the bastion (or Achilles heel) of WMPTE's open platform, half-cab bus operation. It was finally withdrawn in the autumn of 1978. (D. R. Harvey Collection)

252 (VWK 252)

Opposite above: Speeding along Pershore Road in the late nineteenth-century shopping area of Cotteridge, Birmingham, in July 1977 is 252 (VWK 252). This bus had been transferred to WMPTE's South Division within a few months of the take-over, repainted at Tyburn Road Works and renumbered 1252. The Coventry buses were transferred to replace some of the more decrepit Birmingham Standards on the Outer Circle 11 route that were between four and eight years older than these lightweight-bodied Daimler CVG6s. 252 is working on the 11C route and immediately after it has passed the entrance to Cotteridge Bus Garage on the right it will turn right into Watford Road. It would survive in service until the Outer Circle service became the last route to convert from crew-operated half-cab buses, which occurred on 31 October 1977. It was sold to Rollinson of Barnsley for scrap during July 1978. (D. R. Harvey)

254 (VWK 254)

Above: Having been repainted in blue and cream in the spring of 1975 and renumbered 254Y, VWK 254 was quickly transferred to WMPTE's North Division to operate services from Dudley Garage. This was in order to replace former Midland Red buses taken over by the PTE on 3 December 1973. Many of these buses were non-standard BMMO types and were often inherited from Midland Red in a poor state of repair. This sixty-seater Metro-Cammell-bodied Daimler CVG6 is parked outside the Churchill Shopping Precinct in Birmingham Street, Dudley, and is loading up for a 247 route trip to Wednesbury. (L. Mason)

255 (VWK 255)

Above: About to leave The Burges and cross Hales Street and enter Bishop Street on 3 July 1960 behind a Commer Express Delivery 10 cwt van is the two-year-old 255 (VWK 255). Burges is a corruption of 'between the bridges', as it stood between the bridges over the Sherbourne and Radford brooks. The Metro-Cammell Orion sixty-seat Daimler CVG6 is working on the long 20 route to Bedworth. Following the bus is an Austin A70 Hereford with a large four-cylinder 2,199cc engine, a model that was in production from 1951 until 1954. Further back up The Burges are two more Coventry Transport buses, the nearer one being the 1959-built 270 (XVC 270), working on the 11 route, and the just visible Daimler CVD6 147 (KVC 147). Most of the buildings at the bottom end of The Burges escaped bomb damage during the Second World War and those on the left have frontages dating from the eighteenth century. The public house on the right on the corner of Corporation Street was known as the Wine Lodge from 1881 until 10 June 1968, when it was renamed the Tally Ho. It had been built in 1874 as the Eagle Vaults and from 1990 has been known as the Tudor Rose. (R. F. Mack)

257 (VWK 257)

Opposite above: Parked in Black Prince Avenue, Cheylesmore, is Daimler CVG6 257 (VWK 257). It is preparing to return to its city terminus in Broadgate. This Metro-Cammell-bodied bus is operating on the 2 route on 25 January 1960. There is just one passenger on board who has been allowed on the bus, which has the welcome addition of both cab and saloon heaters, rather than stand at the so-called bus shelter, which offered virtually no protection at this somewhat bleak and exposed spot. The conductor is preparing his ticket machine and money bag for the return journey on what appears to be a cold January day. (C. W. Routh)

263 (VWK 263)

Above: Bradney Green off Charter Avenue is near to Tile Hill railway station and was part of the early post-war estate built with prefabricated municipal houses. The Metro-Cammell-bodied Daimler CVG6 bus, 263 (VWK 263), delivered in November 1958, is working on the 18 route and is about to return to its city terminus in Corporation Street. The original bus service from Pool Meadow to Burton Green had been taken over in April 1936 from Bunty Motorways and this was gradually moved outwards along Charter Avenue in three post-war extensions. (C. W. Routh)

265 (VWK 265)

265 (VWK 265), in its alter guise as 265Y, was the last of the 1958 batch of fifty Daimler CVG6s with MCCW Orion bodywork to be delivered and survived in the city under WMPTE ownership until 1978. It was painted in the last livery scheme of the Corporation and is in Pool Meadow bus station in company with a number of former Coventry Daimler Fleetlines with a variety of bodywork. It is leaving the bus station when working on the 7 service to Sewall Highway, with yet again, most of the passengers sitting downstairs. Behind the bus almost hidden by the trees is the medieval Priory Gate. (D. R. Harvey Collection)

401 (XRW 401)

Coventry Transport was quite unusual for a municipality in that it held licenses to operate excursions and private hire work outside the city boundary. This not only allowed for limited trips to seaside resorts and a quick run down the A5 to London but also for 'Aunty Mabel's seventieth birthday trip' or a local fishing club to go to the nearby River Avon. Anyway, the permutations were limitless and although not a front-line activity, initially three of the pre-war Daimler COG5/40s were fitted with semi-coach seats for these duties. In 1954, three of the 1949 Brush-bodied Daimler CVD6 single-deckers were equipped with coach seats but, even though they were kept in immaculate condition, by 1959 any half-cab vehicle parked on a distant coach park was beginning to look a little anachronistic. The result was that Coventry Transport ordered three coaches rather than convert existing buses. These were Daimler 'Freeline' G6H/Ss, which was surprising as Daimler was bringing production of this heavyweight, underfloor-engined chassis to a close. They had Willowbrook Viking C41F bodywork and were very heavy at 7 tons 8 cwt. This trio were the only Gardner-engined 'Freeline' coaches to be operated in the United Kingdom, being fitted with the horizontal version of the Gardner 6HLW 8.4-litre unit. Leaving Pool Meadow bus station on a bus service to Eastern Green is 401 (XRW 401), by now in its new guise, sporting its fleet number. In the background, above the parked Coventry Transport double-deckers, is the north end of St Michael's cathedral, designed by Sir Basil Spence, built in red sandstone and consecrated in 1962. (D. R. Harvey Collection)

402 (XRW 402)

Above: Parked alongside an imported 1947 Packard Clipper sedan carrying a 1958 Middlesex registration is 402 (XRW 402). This Daimler Freeline is being used on a private hire in about 1960 as the driver occupies himself by reading a newspaper in order to pass the time. The Willowbrook Viking coach body had all the elements of an attractive design, but it was rather like the late Eric Morecambe's comment 'but not necessarily in the right order!' Heavily styled with an almost Continental-type windscreen, a glazed pair of rear corner pillars, rubber mounted saloon windows and with a high waistrail, the body type did not receive an excessive number of orders, although BET Group members Devon General and Northern General as well as Birch Brothers did order some. It was built in cooperation with its original owner, Viking Motors of Burton-on-Trent, and was therefore given the model name 'Viking'. (D. R. Harvey Collection)

267 (XVC 267)

Opposite below: Fresh out of Sandy Lane Garage bus wash, 267 (XVC 267) is the second of the 1959 batch of MCCW Orion-bodied Daimler CVG6s. There were twenty-five of these buses, which had the luxury of cab and saloon heaters and were 7 tons 6 cwt. 267 was either freshly painted or wet when this photograph was taken. The maroon and ivory livery looked very smart. Even the Manchester-style concealed radiator looked neat, but as with the previous VWK-registered buses they only had the Daimler monogram on the radiator rather than the curved fluted radiator decoration, which gave them something of a denuded appearance. (L. Mason)

403 (XRW 403)

Above: Between 1965 and 1967, 401–403, although in the sky blue and ivory coach livery, were transferred to bus work and were used on the Berkswell route among others. They were made redundant by the purchase of three Bedford SB5s with Duple C41F bodies in 1964. These were much lighter, more fuel efficient and considerably faster than the Freelines, which could only achieve around 43 mph. 403 (XRW 403) is parked in front of the traffic inspector's hut in Pool Meadow in August 1965, displaying EASTERN GREEN but still retaining the accoutrements of a coach, including a full set of antimacassars. (L. Mason)

268 (XVC 268)

Standing in Earl Street at the bus stop for the 1 route to Stoke Heath is Daimler CVG6 268 (XVC 268). This sixty-seater was delivered to Coventry in October 1959. Alongside the bus are the original premises of the Herbert Art Gallery and Museum, begun in 1939 but only finally opened in 1960. The museum is named after the philanthropist Sir Alfred Herbert, founder of a Coventry-based machine tool company. The museum was totally replaced by a £14 million state-of-the-art building in 2008. Towering in the distance above the bus is the early fifteenth-century Perpendicular tower of Coventry Cathedral, which was the only part of St Michael's church to survive the bombing of Coventry on the night of 14 November 1940. To the rear of the bus is the 1920s-built Tudor-styled Council House that was constructed during the First World War but was only opened on 11 June 1920 by the then Duke of York. (D. R. Harvey Collection)

270 (XVC 270)

Travelling down Trinity Street in the days when it was still a two-way street, from the distant post-war replacement multi-storey Owen Owen department store, is 270 (XVC 270). Owen Owen, which dominated the Broadgate/Trinity Street corner, was the most prestigious shop in Coventry, boasting that it was the first shop to have escalators in the city. This Daimler CVG6 has the usual lightweight sixty-seat body built by Metro-Cammell and is opposite the temporary Sainsbury store, which was replaced in 1960, and is working on the 22 route to Purcell Road. Overtaking the parked Ford Anglia 100E two-door saloon car and following the bus is a Vauxhall Victor F saloon dating from about 1957. (D. Williams)

274 (XVC 274)

Above: Speeding past the old Edwardian central fire station in Hales Street is 274 (XVC 274). The building had been left isolated by the construction of the Swanswell section of the Ringway which had resulted in the demolition of the Gothic-styled St Michael's School and the removal of most of Ford Street. The bus is working on the 9 route and is on its way to Broadgate. The bus has the city crest on the front panel above the destination box and is painted in the final livery used by the Corporation that had been introduced in 1970. (R. F. Mack)

276 (XVC 276)

Opposite below: The late-Victorian villas in the vicinity of the railway station became prime real estate by the mid-1960s and many a high-quality house in Eaton, Park and Manor roads was demolished to make way for office blocks. This has happened to the large stone bay double-fronted house, which is already without its roof. 276 (XVC 276), of November 1959, is operating on the clockwise 14A Inner Circle route and stands at the Eaton Road terminus in 1963. Gradually the area was redeveloped in conjunction with the completion of the rebuilding of the station in 1962 prior to the electrification of the Birmingham to London main line. As per usual for an 8-foot-wide bus, the steering wheel of 276 is white, although once the last of the narrower 7-foot, 6-inch-wide buses had been withdrawn, old black replacements were used. (R. Wellings)

277 (XVC 277)

Above: Still in full Coventry Transport colours but rearranged to conform to the standard West Midlands livery style, 277 was renumbered in the WMPTE fleet number series as 277Y. In 1974 XVC 277 enters Broadgate from Trinity Street. It is working on the 20 route from Bedworth and is overtaking a parked East Lancs-bodied Daimler Fleetline. The bus has the later Daimler 'fluted eyebrow' radiator grill decoration, which does enhance the appearance of the vehicle. Behind the bus is the mock Tudor building originally called Priory Gate; by this time the ground floor shop had become a Wimpy Bar. (A. D. Broughall)

279 (XVC 279)

Above: On a miserable looking day, the bus turning from Trinity Street into Ironmonger Row in front of the Owen Owen store in the heart of Coventry's city centre is 279 (XVC 279), a 1959-delivered, Metro-Cammell-bodied Daimler CVG6. This bus is working on the Keresley Road service number 16A route. The Priory Gate building of 1938 is still occupied by the chemists Timothy White & Taylor. The bus is being followed by a Mini and a Hillman Minx Series II four-door saloon. Parked in the shadow of Holy Trinity church is an earlier CVG6, which is on the 20 route. (R. F. Mack)

280 (XVC 280)

Opposite above: The large number of young children congregating outside the Coventry Theatre has just seen a production of *The Wizard of Oz*. A rather well-loaded 280 (XVC 280) turns around the corner in front of the theatre in Hales Street when working on the 9 route to Copsewood. Behind the bus in Hales Street is the large Smithfield Tavern, with the impressive Bass sign above the entrance. This pub was built on the site of Coventry's original cattle market in 1862 in a four-storey mock Tudor style. It was later known as the Smithfield Hotel and was demolished in 2010 after being gutted by fire. (D. R. Harvey Collection)

281 (XVC 281)

Above: Although it looked like any other of Coventry's Gardner-engined Daimlers, 281 (XVC 281) was fitted with the almost extinct Daimler CD6 8.6-litre engine. This engine had been officially been out of production since 1954 and in its Mark VIII form was only used in five Alexander-bodied buses for Glasgow Corporation in November 1959 and three delivered in April 1960 with Weymann bodies to Swindon Corporation. Although built as a CVG6, the chassis of 281 was re-engined prior to being despatched from Daimlers and was as a consequence delivered late in February 1960. Behind the bus is Keresley Road, which was part of the then A423 that was the main road from Tamworth to south of Oxford by way of Coventry. 281 is working in the inbound 15 service and is being followed by an Austin A90 Atlantic car. (A. D. Broughall)

285 (XVC 285)

The bus parked in Pool Meadow bus station on the 23 service for Allesley Park is Daimler CVG6 285 (XVC 285). Allesley is in the north-west of the city, just north of the A45 Dunchurch Highway and east of Birmingham Road, and still retains its original village character. The Birmingham Road which originally ran through the village was part of Thomas Telford's toll road from London to Holyhead and was opened in 1824. In the interwar period the village began to be linked towards Coventry by 'ribbon development' along the main roads, while during the 1950s the first development of green land at nearby Allesley Park began. As a consequence the 23 service was introduced in May 1959 when the estate was barely completed. (A. D. Broughall)

289 (XVC 289)

On a rainy day in about 1960, bus 289 (XVC 289) squelches down The Burges towards Corporation Street. It has just passed the Coventry Cross public house. This building has been variously claimed to date from the sixteenth or seventeenth century, although the frontage is late Georgian. The pub stands above the culverted River Sherbourne. The bus is a Daimler CVG6 with a Metro-Cammell H33/27R body and is operating on the 18A service to Canley. Towering above the bus in the distance is the back of the Owen Owen department store, while behind the bus is a Ford Prefect dating from around 1950. (R. F. Mack)

291 (291 RW)

Above: The first of the 1961 batch of Daimler CVG6 was 291 (291 RW), but, unlike the rest of the twenty-two buses, this one arrived at WMPTE on 1 April 1974 as a withdrawn vehicle. It was being converted to a tree lopper prior to the takeover, by the simple expedient of the removal of the upper saloon structures and roof. It was renumbered 015 and first used in May 1974 and in January 1984 as 414 went for scrap. It is travelling around the back of Wheatley Street Garage adjacent to Pool Meadow bus station with the ring road flyover just visible. The bus is displaying the somewhat politically correct legend 'PLANT MAINTENANCE'. (W. J. Haynes)

292 (292 RW)

Opposite above: Travelling on the 1 route to Chapelfields is 292 (292 RW), still with its original white roof. Delivered during August 1961, these Daimler CVG6s had fluid friction clutches with pre-selector gearboxes while the Metro-Cammell bodies had an increased seating capacity with a H34/29R body. Despite this, the buses weighed 6 tons 19 cwt, which was 7 cwt lighter than the previous buses. The 1 route had its terminus in the city centre outside the Council House and crossed Hearsall Common on its way to Allesley Old Road. A Midland Red LD8 comes through the tree-lined road and draws up behind the Austin Loadstar 5-tonner. Behind the Austin A55 Farina-styled car travelling towards the city centre is a KVC-registered Daimler CVD6 also operating on the 1 route. (W. J. Haynes)

293 (293 RW)

Above: Travelling along Hales Street is 293 (293 RW), on its way to the city terminus in Broadgate by way of Trinity Street. The cream roof painted bus is passing the premises of Matterson, Huxley & Watson's ironmonger's shop, while located behind that was their iron and brass foundry. 293 is working on the 2 route to Cheylesmore and is a standard Coventry Daimler CVG6 with a Metro Cammell H34/29R body and sports the Daimler 'eyebrow' fluting on the front of the bonnet cowling. This bus would pass to WMPTE in April 1974, becoming 293Y, and was withdrawn at the end of 1977. (D. R. Harvey Collection)

294 (294 RW)

Above: Daimler CVG6 294 (294 RW), with the usual Orion-style Metro-Cammell bodywork, is virtually empty as it travels past the 1920s-built Council House in Earl Street. It has just left its terminus and will proceed via High Street, Hertford Street, Warwick Road, Spencer Road, and eventually on to Allesley Old Road and its terminus at Chapelfields. Behind the bus in the distance is Jordan Well, with another bus waiting in the bus lay-by. With their unladen weight of just under 7 tons and their Gardner 6LW 8.4-litre engines, what these buses lost in creature comforts for the sixty-three passengers they made up for in reliability and fuel economy, which by the 1960s was becoming of great importance to all bus operators across the country. (R. F. Mack)

297 (297 RW)

Opposite above: Parked in Pool Meadow bus station when between duties on the 23 service is 297 (297 RW). These twenty-two Daimler CVG6s had a Gardner 6LW 8.4-litre engine coupled to a fluid friction clutch with a pre-selector gearbox. The sixty-three-seat Metro-Cammell Orion body weighed only 6 tons 19 cwt but despite its utilitarian looks provided comfortable seating and the luxury of saloon and cab heaters. The ivory upper saloon window surrounds and roof made the maroon look considerably less dowdy for the intending passengers and was the first stage in reducing the amount of maroon when the rear-engined buses were introduced in 1965. (C. D. Mann)

300 (300 RW)

Above: Turning from Hales Street into Trinity Street is 300 (300 RW). This Daimler CVG6 with its MCCW Orion body is working on the 11 route to Willenhall and, as was frequently the case out of the peak periods in Coventry, the lower saloon is full of passengers while the upper saloon is virtually empty. The advertisement for Co-operative shopping was a common one at the beginning of the 1960s. Behind the bus on the corner of Trinity Street is an early Thornton's Chocolate Kabin whose products were distinctly more 'upmarket' than chocolates made in Bournville, Bristol or York. Behind the Ford Anglia Standard 105E, with the narrow radiator grill, is Matterson, Huxley & Watson's ironmonger's shop in Hales Street. (P. M. Photography)

302 (302 RW)

Standing in Broadgate when working on the 22 route is 302 (302 RW). This route to Willenhall was introduced in July 1956 as the cross-city extension to the Sewall Highway service. It is passing the temporary shops which by this date had as one of the many occupants a City Information shop for the emerging post-war tourist trade. This Daimler CVG6 bus entered service in August 1961 and its Metro-Cammell Orion lightweight body looks more modern when compared to the body built by the same manufacturer some nine years later on a KVC-registered Daimler CVD6 parked behind 302. Towering over the buses is the fifteenth-century, 237-foot-high tower and spire of Holy Trinity parish church. (P. M. Photography)

303 (303 RW)
Turning out of Broadgate in about 1970 with the Leofric Hotel to the rear and the Owen Owen department store on the right is Daimler CVG6 303 (303 RW), with the cream roof livery and the small fleet name above the municipal crest on its Metro-Cammell body. It is empty and is turning into Trinity Street while running back to Sandy Lane Garage having just overtaken 41 (KKV 41G), the first of the 1969-built East Lancs-bodied Daimler Fleetline CRG6LXs. In its original post-war guise Broadgate was around sixteen years old and the trees in the large traffic island in its middle had reached near maturity, affording some modesty to Lady Godiva, whose statue graced this central grassed area. (A. J. Douglas)

306 (306 RW)

Above: The 9 route to Earlsdon was introduced in October 1937 after the closure of the 8 tram service. The bus route had its terminus in Broadgate, in front of Holy Trinity parish church. 306 (306 RW) stands in front of the temporary shops as it awaits its departure time. The bus, one of the twenty-two buses delivered in August and September 1961, was identifiable as a Harnall Lane Garage vehicle and is painted in the WMPTE livery layout though the lower panels and roof were painted in Marshall Red rather than West Midlands Oxford Blue. After January 1974, this colour scheme was replaced by the standard West Midlands PTE blue and cream. (J. C. Walker)

309 (309 RW)

Opposite below: Cream-roofed 309 (309 RW) waits at the traffic lights in Corporation Street at the junction with The Burges. In the 1960s traffic congestion was for most of the day at a minimum so hopping on and off a bus with an open back platform was a well-practiced skill, as exemplified by the man in the carriageway. This Daimler CVG6 is coming back into the city centre from Keresley. The bus is passing the mock Tudor frontage of the Wine Lodge public house, which dated from 1874. This pub was tied to Truman's Brewery, which was based in east London. Following bus 309 is a 1965 Hillman Imp, one of the great near misses of the British car industry; it had a Coventry Climax-based 875cc rear engine and a superb gearbox but was cursed with a poor build quality. (F. W. York)

312 (312 RW)

Above: On 24 June 1969, when Trinity Street had been converted to a one-way route, three very similar Manchester-fronted Daimler CVG6s, all with Metro-Cammell bodies, climb up Trinity Street from Hales Street towards Broadgate. Leading the front row of the rugby scrum is the white-roofed 312 (312 RW), working on the 21 route to Wood End. Speeding up the hill in the tighthead prop forward position is 235 (VWK 235) on the 13 route, while bringing up the rear as the loosehead prop is 226, another of the VWK-registered buses on the 9 route to Earlsdon. (A. J. Douglas)

7000 HP

Above: The revolutionary rear-engined Daimler Fleetline was developed during 1958 and 1959 and the prototype was intended for Birmingham City Transport. Registered 7000 HP, it was demonstrated to BCT in their livery from 16 December 1960 to 31 January 1961. 7000 HP, now without Birmingham's municipal crests, was on loan to Coventry Transport from Transport Vehicles (Daimler) from 8 to 24 April 1962. It is emerging from Trinity Street, which was converted to a one-way street in the opposite direction in June 1962, and is working on a northbound 22 service to Sewall Highway. Behind the bus in Hales Street is the large Smithfield Tavern, with the impressive Bass sign above the entrance. This pub was built on the site of Coventry's original cattle market in 1862 in a four-storey mock Tudor style. It was later known as the Smithfield Hotel and was demolished in 2010 after being gutted by fire. 7000 HP was eventually sold to Blue Bus of Willington but was burn out in their Repton Road garage fire on 5 January 1976. Parked outside the Coventry Hippodrome is Daimler CVD6 135 (KVC 135), while beyond that is the old fourteenth-century red sandstone chapel used as the three centuries as the Free Grammar School. (D. G. Savage)

SGD 584

Opposite above: SGD 584 was on hire from Leyland Motors from 19 to 25 August 1962 and was used on the 8 route to Tile Hill. This Leyland Atlantean PDR1/1 had a high-capacity Alexander H44/34F body and a rear, transversely mounted Leyland O.600 engine. It was Glasgow Corporation's LA6 and was in their livery of orange lower panels and green above the upper saloon floor level separated by a white strip above the lower saloon windows. The success of the demonstration of this bus led to an order for the twenty Atlantean PDR1/2s delivered in 1964 but with bodies built by Willowbrook in Loughborough. (D. R. Harvey Collection)

314 (314 CRW)

Above: Turning into Hertford Street from Broadgate is 314 (314 CRW). This was the second of the final batch of buses ordered by Mr Ronald Fearnley and had entered service in December 1963, some thirty years after his first purchase, 101 (KV 7101), had been delivered in January 1931. 314 is working on the 9 service to Earlsdon with a very full load which is causing the driver to do some hauling on his steering wheel to get the bus into Hertford Street in the days when power steering was virtually unheard-of. As soon as Mr Fearnley had retired, his successor, Mr Noël McDonald, who had previously been at Warrington Corporation, introduced a new livery that was mainly white with maroon relief and rear-engined buses. Such buses are in and around Broadgate as 314 leaves for the outer suburbs. (C. W. Routh)

316 (316 CRW)

Pool Meadow was not only the Corporation's bus station but alongside it was a large parking area that was used by Midland Red's stage carriage bus services and as a stopping off point for long-distance coach services. It would be too much of a compliment to call it a coach park as it was little more than an ash or sometime gravel-covered area where coaches stopped as close as they could to the mock Tudor Meadow Café at the entrance to the bus station. 316 (316 CRW), a standard Coventry Daimler CVG6, turns right out of the bus station into Ford Street when working on an 8A service to Tile Hill North. (F. W. York)

317 (317 CRW)

Passing Sam Robbin's Austin car dealership and showrooms in Cox Street in about 1969 is 317 (317 CRW), although only the car on the forecourt is an Austin, in this case a 1100. Of the two cars in the showroom, only the one facing the 1100 parked outside is identifiable, a Vauxhall Viva HB saloon. The Metro-Cammell-bodied Daimler CVG6 bus is on the 13 service to Willenhall, terminating on London Road just beyond Chace Avenue. The bus would have left Pool Meadow bus station and come out of the city centre via Ford Street, Cox Street and Whitefriars Street. In the distance is the newly built Swanswell Ringway, which would cut a swath through the Pool Meadow area of inner Coventry and in a stroke caused many interesting buildings to be demolished and their previous footprint left as unused ground or a poorly maintained car park. (A. Wilson)

319 (319 CRW)

Above: Turning out of Ironmonger Row and about to tackle the descent of The Burges is Metro-Cammell-bodied Daimler CVG6 319 (319 CRW). It is working on the 20 route to Longford and is being followed by a Morris Minor 1000 and its near cousin, the Wolseley 1500. Behind them is the large almost curtain brick wall of the rear of the Owen Owen department store, which for all its rows of porthole windows still emphatically looked like a rather unimaginatively designed 1950s building. These last twenty-five Coventry half-cab double-deckers reverted to the older style livery with a maroon roof, making them look distinctly old-fashioned. (F. W. York)

320 (320 CRW)

Opposite above: Having arrived from Bell Green on the 6 route in about 1964, 320 (320 CRW) waits at the bus shelter in Pool Meadow bus station for new passengers who, once on board, would be quickly off on their journey as the service had a 10-minute headway. This sixty-three-seater Daimler CVG6 entered service in November 1963 and would serve the city for fifteen years. The simple layout of the bus station enabled buses operating high-frequency services to drive in, park at their designated stop and then load up and leave without overdue congestion. It might have lacked modern facilities but it was practical and accessible for passengers, something which perhaps its replacement, opened in 1994, has always lacked. (G. Pattison)

322 (322 CRW)

Above: Parked in front of the premises of the Coventry Information Centre in Broadgate in 1974 is 322 (322 CRW). It was not long after this that the 'temporary' shops were demolished. This Harnall Lane-based bus is in the immediate pre-West Midlands PTE takeover livery and numbered 322Y in preparation for the Coventry Transport fleet's absorption. The Daimler CVG6 with its MCCW H34/29R body is working on the 9 route to Earlsdon and is getting very close to being full up with passengers. Behind it is a Neepsend-bodied Daimler Fleetline CRG6LX, 11 (CKV 11D), on the 10 route to Keresley Road. (A. D. Broughall)

325 (325 CRW)

John Anslow's was a high-quality shop selling furniture, carpets, linens, blinds, soft furnishings and bedsteads. It was located in its purpose-built premises, built in 1875, on the corner of High Street and Hay Lane. Travelling past the shop along High Street, displaying 'Canley via Prior Deram Walk' 18A route on the destination blinds, is 325 (325 CRW). This is one of the twenty-five Daimler CVG6s with Metro-Cammell Orion bodies that were delivered at the end of 1963 in the predominantly maroon livery with white window surrounds. Following the bus is a minivan and a large Ford Zephyr 4 Mark IV saloon. (R. F. Mack)

326 (326 CRW)

Speeding along Warwick Road from Hertford Street and travelling towards Coventry railway station is 326 (326 CRW). This Metro-Cammell-bodied Daimler CVG6 is operating on the 9 service to Earlsdon and is wearing the final style of Coventry Transport livery. The bollards in the foreground mark the entrance to Greyfriars while behind the bus is the lovely early nineteenth-century Georgian row of three-storied, Italianate-styled houses. 326 was one of only ten Daimler CVG6s to survive in service in Coventry into 1979. (A. Wilson)

330 (330 CRW)

Above: Buses were rarely photographed leaving Broadgate in the short Trinity Street section before Ironmonger Row, alongside the large Owen Owen department store. 330 (330 CRW), a Daimler CVG6 with a Metro-Cammell H34/29R body, is seen turning into Ironmonger Row when working on the 9 service to Copsewood in the late 1960s. In the background, buses swirl around Broadgate, including a Willowbrook-bodied Leyland Atlantean rear-engined bus. This latter bus has pulled in at the bus stops alongside the prefabricated shops on the east side of Broadgate, with the National Provincial Bank with its classical portico facing the Atlantean. (R. F. Mack)

334 (334 CRW)

Opposite below: Two of the last Daimler CVG6s with Metro-Cammell Orion H34/29R bodywork were preserved after the final demise of half-cab, open rear platform buses in Coventry. 334 (334 CRW) was bought by the Aston Manor Road Transport Museum and was lovingly restored by them back to its original condition. 333 (333 CRW) became the last WMPTE half-cab and was ceremonially pulled into Harnall Lane Garage on 24 August 1979. It was repainted by hand in full Coventry Transport livery in the Corporation's paint shop and then handed over to the Coventry Transport Museum. The result was splendid but the museum advertised itself along the length of the panels between the decks, which can just be seen and rather spoilt the restoration. Both buses are parked in the yard at the side of the lamented Aston Manor Road Transport Museum in Witton on 5 August 2000. (D. R. Harvey)

332 (332 CRW)

Above: The view across Pool Meadow bus station shows the partially redeveloped facility with the old scaffolding style of bus shelter being used in the shadow of the elevated Swanswell Ringway. The perennial newspaper vendor sells a copy of the *Coventry Evening Telegraph* from inside his tiny covered stall while a pair of bus drivers begin to cross the road once the bus has gone past. The bus is 332 (332 CRW), a Metro-Cammell-bodied Daimler CVG6 on its way to Stoke, but is not showing a route number. It has been renumbered 332Y in the WMPTE fleet sequence but is still in Coventry livery although without any municipal crests. (A. D. Broughall)

335 (335 CRW)

Above: Swinging out of Broadgate on the 2 service to Radford is 335 (335 CRW). This Daimler CVG6 is overtaking a still fairly new 367 (CRW 367C), a Daimler Fleetline CRG6LX with a Willowbrook H44/32F body dating from April 1965. There was just a fifteen-month age gap between the two buses and while the CVG6 was preferred by bus enthusiasts and the maintenance staff, passengers, crews and garage staff much preferred the new rear-engined buses. This time difference between the buses would be further reflected in the fact that the CVG6 would be withdrawn in 1978 while the Fleetline went just two years later. (A. J. Douglas)

404 (404 CWK)

Opposite below: In April 1964 Coventry received the first of three Bedford SB5 coaches. They had Duple Bella Vega C41F bodywork painted in light blue and white and had a Bedford 5.42-litre six-cylinder diesel engine. These three were 'genuine' coaches which, although coming from what was considered to be a lightweight chassis manufacturer, had a good turn of speed, were tolerably comfortable to drive even allowing for the four-speed manual gearbox and were fuel efficient. These Bedfords replaced the Daimler Freeline coaches, which were relegated to bus work. 404 (404 CWK) stands in Pool Meadow bus station on 17 March 1967 and would remain in service until sold in 1972 to Primrose Valley of Filey. (Photofives)

337 (337 CRW)

Above: Passing the main booking office of the Coventry-based coach operator Red House Motors, near to the exit at Pool Meadow bus station, is the very last half-cab, open rear platform bus ever purchased by Coventry Transport. 337 (337 CRW), one of Sandy Lane's finest, is a sixty-three-seater Daimler CVG6 with a Metro-Cammell Orion body. Even with its more driver-friendly pre-selector gearbox and fluid friction clutch, the layout of these buses was looking dated and certainly the 'good old reliable' Gardner 6LW 8.4-litre engine was perhaps getting a bit long in the tooth for a modern bus. It is working on the 7 route to Brownshill Green and has already been renumbered 337Y as part of the WMPTE fleet. In the background is the flyover section of Swanswell Ringway, built in 1968. (A. D. Broughall)

501 (CDU 51B)

501 (CDU 51B) was a somewhat surprising choice of vehicle as not only was it a Ford, an unusual 530E model, but it also had a light blue and cream-painted Martin Walker body with a capacity of just twenty-five. The design for this coach had been developed by Kenex of Ashford in Kent but was briefly continued after they were taken over by Martin Walker in 1964. Two similar, though slightly smaller, coaches were delivered to Wolverhampton Corporation on Ford 529E chassis but were genuine Kenex products and had the model name 'Romney'. The Coventry vehicle had a four-cylinder, 3.6-litre diesel engine and was purchased to nominally supplement the three Bedford Duple coaches as well as to be available to transport disabled school children, though with a narrow three-step entrance it must have made access for some of them a little awkward. (D. R. Harvey Collection)

405 (CDU 405B)

Parked in Harnall Lane Garage is the second of the three Bedford SB5s with Duple Bella Vega C41F bodies. The Bella Vega body, or Trooper if mounted on a Ford Thames chassis, was a very popular body, even if the somewhat quirky sloping side pillar was not to everyone's taste. 405 (CDU 405B) was delivered to the Corporation in January 1964 and had an eight-year operational life with Coventry. They were used on 'proper' coaching duties and were never used or converted for stage carriage work. All three were sold to Primrose Valley Coaches of Filey. (R. H. G. Simpson)

The Rear-Engined Era up to the West Midland PTE Takeover

343 (CDU 343B)

In WMPTE ownership but painted in Coventry's Marshall Red and Shetland ivory livery is 343 (CDU 343B). This Willowbrook-bodied Leyland Atlantean PDR1/2 entered service in January 1965 and had a service life of fifteen years. Allocated to Harnall Lane Garage, it is leaving Pool Meadow bus station when working on the 3 route to Holbrooks. Although Willowbrook double-deckers were less common after about 1958, these buses were the Loughborough-based coachbuilder's first rear-engined, double-decker bodies, but like their predecessors were perhaps not quite as durable as the products of other manufacturing. By this time, about 1975, the destination boxes had been reconstructed with just a route number box and a single line blind aperture. (D. R. Harvey Collection)

344 (CDU 344B)

The new style Willowbrook body was a radical departure when compared to the products of Metro-Cammell, Northern Counties and Park Royal, who had modified their bodies on front-engined chassis for both Daimler Fleetline and Leyland Atlantean chassis. The body had very little in common with their products mounted on half-cab buses, with only the rear dome and upper saloon emergency entrance resembling their earlier products. The front of the bus was quite flat and had large twin windscreens while the sides of the upper saloon were slightly cranked inwards. The result was an attractive looking bus, especially in their original livery. 344 (CDU 344B), one of the PDR1/2s, stands in Pool Meadow bus station when working on the 7 route to Sewall Highway in about 1966. This bus had been fitted with an additional ventilator in the front dome. (C. D. Mann)

345 (CDU 345B)

Above: Coventry Transport's first order for rear-engined buses went to Leyland in 1963 because of a keenly priced tender and because, with the need to keep the overall height down, the order was placed for the PDR1/2, which had central gangways throughout each deck. This version of the Atlantean was fitted with the Daimler-built concentric drive gearbox as used on the Fleetline and a dropped-centre, double-reduction rear axle that was used in the Albion Lowlander. Daimler-Jaguar bought their major castings from West Yorkshire Foundries, a Leyland subsidiary, and thus the PDR1/2 model could be fitted with a Daimler semi-automatic gearbox coupled to a fluid friction lock-up clutch. Willowbrook-bodied 345 (CDU 345B) crosses from its dropping off point in front of Trinity church into Broadgate, where it will pick up passengers on the 15 route to Whitmore Park, a service that was introduced in June 1958. (D. R. Harvey Collection)

352 (CDU 352B)

Opposite above: A Willowbrook-bodied Leyland Atlantean PDR1/2 passes into Broadgate from Trinity Street. Except for the design of the rear engine cover, there was very little to differentiate between the Willowbrook bodies on the Atlantean and Fleetline chassis. 352 (CDU 352B) is another of the twenty-two of the contentious order that was delivered despite local objections in which the Jaguar-Daimler concern, local politicians and the trade unions found themselves on common ground and co-operating in fighting. It is working on the 21 route having arrived from Wood End in the north of the city. Behind the bus is the mid-1950s retail block occupied by the Owen Owen department store. On the left is a Standard Vanguard III, a 2.1-litre, four-cylinder saloon that was only in production between 1956 and 1958. The bus is in its original condition, having been delivered in January 1965, and was withdrawn in 1980. (R. Marshall)

353 (CDU 353B)

Above: Flanked on the skyline by the spired towers of Holy Trinity parish church on the right, behind the multi-storey car park, and that of the Cathedral of St Michael adjacent to the nave of Basil Spence's 1962 construction is Coventry Transport's 353 (CDU 353B). This Leyland Atlantean PDR1/2 has a Willowbrook H44/32F body and is standing in Pool Meadow bus station at the time when it was aligned at right angles to Fairfax Street in the mid-1960s. The bus has just arrived in the bus station having worked into the city on the 13 service from Ryton, a service that did not operate on Sundays. (D. R. Harvey Collection)

355 (CDU 355B)

Above: Prior to disposal, withdrawn buses were usually parked in out-of-the-way plots of land alongside garages where prying eyes, bus enthusiasts and souvenir hunters could not easily find them. Close examination of withdrawn 355 (CDU 355B) shows that the Willowbrook body on this Leyland Atlantean has already been cannibalised: both the front windows are missing their glass and the front dome is damaged. The bus, renumbered 355Y, is missing its destination blinds and the license holder is empty. The bus was withdrawn in early 1980 and was awaiting collection by the bus dealer Booth of Rotherham, which would occur in June 1980. An engineless 300 (300 RW), a Daimler CVG6, would go to Rollinson of Barnsley in June 1979. (D. R. Harvey)

358 (CDU 358B)

Opposite below: The Leyland Atlantean PDR1/2 was fitted with the smaller Leyland o.600 9.8-litre engine which was the only option because of torque limitations on the rear axle, driving through a friction clutch. The o.600 engine in a bus weighing 8 tons 7 cwt meant that the engine was usually operating at the top end of its performance. The larger 11.1-litre o.680 engine, advertised as 'the Power Plus', was used in some versions of the Atlantean chassis. The PDR1/2s were among the first Atlanteans to feature a dropped rear axle as a flat floor had been specified. The bustle at the rear of the bus was easily identifiable from the Daimler Fleetline by the three-sided bottom support piece that was part of the structure supporting the engine and gearbox. 358 (CDU 359B), with a Willowbrook H44/32F body, approaches the terminus of the 21 route when new in 1965. (L. Mason)

360 (CRW 360C)

Above: Parked at the terminus of the 21 route in Wood End is the first of the Willowbrook-bodied Daimler Fleetline CRG6LXs delivered in March 1965. The early post-war housing in this north-eastern Coventry municipal estate was a June 1957 extension of the old tram service 5 to Bell Green, going to Wood End via Hall Green Road and Hillmorton Road. As with the slightly earlier Atlanteans, these new high-capacity vehicles, numbered 360–381, introduced a revised livery in which cream was the main colour, with the addition of three thick maroon bands around the body. The two front destination boxes were larger and now placed centrally one on top of the other, with a separate route number box at the nearside. (L. Mason)

366 (CRW 366C)

Opposite: 366 (CRW 366C) travels along White Street when new in 1965 as it comes into the city centre on its way to Willenhall from Purcell Road on the 22 route. Behind the bus is Swanswell (or Priory) Gate. This was part of the fourteenth-century city wall, which encircled the medieval town. It was nearly 2.2 miles long and was made up of two parallel 12-foot-high red sandstone walls, 8 feet thick, infilled with rubble. It had thirty-two towers and twelve gatehouses allowing access into the town. Coventry was an important market town whose trades were strictly controlled by guilds. The bus is being followed by a Ford Anglia 105E saloon. (D. R. Harvey Collection)

367 (CRW 367C)

Above: The 3 route to Stoke Aldermoor started outside the Alexandra Cinema in Ford Street, just 'a stone's throw' from Pool Meadow bus station. 367 (CRW 367C), an almost new Willowbrook-bodied Leyland Atlantean PDR1/2, begins to swallow up the queue of intending passengers at the bus shelter for the 3 route. The only major difference between the Willowbrook bodies on the two types of rear-engined chassis was that those on the Daimler Fleetlines had an extra pair of sliding ventilators in each saloon. It is worth observing that the 'flag' for the bus stop is at the back end of the shelter, thus being intended for rear-entrance buses. The driver of 367 has had to stop at the normal boarding point, resulting in most of his bus being on the roadway before the stop. (D. R. Harvey Collection)

368 (CRW 368C)

Above: The twenty-two Daimler Fleetline CRG6LX chassis with Willowbrook seventy-six-seater bodies, numbered 360–381, were well-appointed vehicles though the seating in both saloons was finished in red vynide instead of the earlier moquette. They had fluid flywheels and semi-automatic gearboxes which tended to produce a smoother gear change than those achieved on the Atlanteans. 368 (CRW 368C) picks up passengers outside the Owen Owen department store in Broadgate when being employed on the 15 service to Whitmore Park in about 1973, as the bus is painted in the predominantly ivory and Marshall Red livery. (D. R. Harvey Collection)

371 (CRW 371C)

Opposite above: The number of variations of livery worn by both the Leyland Atlanteans and the Daimler Fleetlines during their operating life was surprisingly large and 371 (CRW 371C) wears yet another variation. The Marshall Red and Shetland ivory livery had been introduced during 1970 and well over half of the fleet had been repainted by the end of 1973. When West Midlands PTE took over Coventry Transport on 1 April 1974, they inherited a bus fleet that was not desperately in need of repainting and so the vynide WM WEST MIDLANDS fleet name was applied on a Marshall Red ground. 371 stands in Corporation Street in 1974 when working on the 13 route across the city from Broad Lane to Willenhall via the bus station. (D. R. Harvey Collection)

373 (CRW 373C)

Above: Broadgate became both the picking up and setting down point for many of the Corporation bus services, including the 2, 13, 15, 21 and 22 routes, which all had loading stands in front of the Owen Owen store. Behind the two buses is the Leofric Hotel, named after the eleventh-century Earl of Mercia who, as well as being a well-respected ruler over this large tract of Saxon Midlands England, was husband to Lady Godiva, whose equestrian exploits are well recorded both in fact and in legend. Both buses are Willowbrook-bodied Daimler Fleetline CRG6LXs led by 373 (CRW 373C), working on the 2 route to Radford, where its chassis had been constructed, followed by 373 (CRW 379C), about to leave the city centre on the 13 to Whitmore Park. (A. J. Douglas)

378 (CRW 378C)

Above: 378Y (CRW 378C) stands, with nearly all its windows smashed, in Liverpool Street Garage yard in Birmingham after withdrawal in early 1979. It sits in the yard in company with withdrawn Birmingham Fleetlines, scrap tyres, engine parts and the detritus of a dumping ground soaked in leaked engine oil. This bus, once the pride of the Coventry Transport fleet, will soon be towed away by Booth, a Rotherham PSV scrap merchant, in June 1979. (D. R. Harvey Collection)

375 (CRW 375C)

Opposite above: Parked in Pool Meadow bus station, alongside the little shed that sold cigarettes, is 375 (CRW 375C). This Willowbrook-bodied Daimler Fleetline CRG6LX has still got the patina of a new bus as it waits for its driver to return before working on the 13 service to Ryton. At 8 tons 8 cwt, the Fleetlines weighed only one hundredweight more than the Atlanteans but, with their large 10.45-litre Gardner 6LX engines, had a better power-to-weight ratio. As was usual in the bus station, 375 has been parked at its shelter while the crew went on their break, most likely a for a cup of tea and a fag. After a suitable time they would come back to their charge which, as it was fitted with doors, was empty as intending passengers could not board, unlike the 'good old days' when the buses had open back platforms. (J. C. Walker)

380 (CRW 380C)

Above: In its pomp, Willowbrook-bodied Daimler Fleetline 380 (CRW 380C) leaves Pool Meadow bus station and is about to turn right into Fairfax Street. The bus is working to the north-west of the city on the 7 route to Allesley. The bus is passing the old Meadow Café in about 1969 as the newly constructed Swanswell Ringway flyover still looks pristine. The bus is working as a one-man-operated vehicle as the two notices above the entrance, 'CASH AND PASSES' and 'TICKET HOLDERS', were intended to direct boarding passengers to either pay or gain access to the bus and not clog up the platform area. (J. C. Walker)

504 (CRW 504C)

Parked off Fairfax Street is 504 (CRW 504C). This was one of the seven Bedford VAS1 single-deckers fitted with Marshall B30F bodywork. The Marshall bodywork was given the name 'Cambretta', which, bearing in mind that Marshall's were based in Cambridge, was supposed to mean 'Little Cambridge', but sounded more like a make of Italian scooter! These buses were licensed for PSV operation but were primarily purchased for the special schools services provided for disabled children. They entered service in July 1965 when the Transport Department took over this operation from the Coventry Social Services Department. They were replaced by the smaller Commer BFD 3023 Walker-bodied twelve-seaters and were gradually turned over to bus services such as the 14 and 19 that had lighter loaded passenger numbers. (R. F. Mack)

506 (CRW 506C)

On 28 November 1966, Coventry Transport introduced its first one-man-operation service from the railway station to Pool Meadow. Numbered 25, the route had a 10-minute headway and used 505 and 506 of the Marshall-bodied Bedford VAS1s which carried CITY-RAILBUS side-mounted slip boards. The 25 railway station to Pool Meadow bus service became very popular as Coventry station, although served by other Transport Department bus routes, is located on the south side of the ring road and is realistically too far to walk to from the city centre. This Bedford VAS1 with a Marshall body, now down-seated by one to B29F, is fully loaded as it turns out of Station Square on its way back to the city centre and on to Pool Meadow bus station. The Marshall bodywork was derived from a type supplied to the British military in the early 1960s and in bus form was supplied to operators mainly in rural areas. In Coventry the buses soon proved unsuitable for normal service work as they were too small and they were too big for the school special-needs work. As a result the seven buses were all sold between 1968 and 1973 to independent operators in areas such as Herefordshire, Shropshire, Weardale and even Waterford in the Irish Republic. (D. R. Harvey Collection)

508 (CRW 508C)

Above: The 19 route to Berkswell to the west of the city had been acquired from Bunty Motorways in April 1936. It had always been a lightly loaded route and operated an hourly service from Pool Meadow bus station. It is in the bus station on a distinctly miserable looking day that 508 (CRW 508C) stands, with its driver issuing tickets to the boarding passengers. These Marshall-bodied Bedford VAS1s had Bedford's own 4.92-litre engine, which was more than adequate for this small-capacity bus. It was almost like history repeating itself as the VAS1s were similar in size to the wartime Bedford OWBs of 1942 and worked on the more lightly loaded routes. (D. R. Harvey Collection)

512 (CRW 512C)

Opposite above: In the late spring of 1965, with the need to expand the school children's special needs bus fleet, while using smaller vehicles, seven twelve-seaters were ordered. These were based on the Commer BFD3023 30 cwt chassis, which had a 10-foot, 4-inch wheelbase and a Rootes 2.26-litre diesel engine. The body was basically a large delivery van converted to a fully equipped PSV that was supplied by Walker, of Dormobile fame. Displaying the route letter L, 512 (CRW 512C) of June 1965 turns out of The Burges and into Hales Street at 2.48 p.m. on the afternoon of 29 August 1969. With the driver is a chaperone who assisted the children on and off the bus; these Walker-bodied Commer BFD3023 buses had a sliding entrance door and the accoutrements of a much larger vehicle. They did not, however, have the advantage of being fitted with a destination blind and had to make do with made up numbers or cards which related to the route to the houses of the children who needed picking up and then taken to their specific school. (A. J. Douglas)

523 (KDU 523D)

Above: These buses were introduced to expand the special schools services taken over by the undertaking from other departments of the Corporation. A rather battered-looking 523 (KDU 523D) was the second one of a pair of Walker B12F-bodied Commer BFD3023s that entered service in November 1966 and, like all these small buses, always looked a little 'uncertain' on their single rear wheels. They were licensed as PSVs but were rarely used on anything else other than school contracts and the occasional private hire. 523 had been working on the H school run. (A. J. Owen)

CRH 175C

Above: Leyland Panther PSUR1/1 CRH 175C was on loan for three weeks from 12 July 1965 until 2 August 1965. The bus was demonstrated by Leyland Motors prior to entering service with Kingston-upon-Hull Corporation as their 175 in July 1965. This was 175's last outing as a demonstrator, having previously been on hire to both Chesterfield and West Hartlepool Corporations. The rear-engined bus had a Leyland o.600 engine and was bodied by Roe with a body using a dual-door layout and seating for forty-four. Like many of the first generation of rear-engined, single-deck buses, the Panther proved to be unreliable and no orders for the Panther were placed. The bus is operating on the 14 Inner Circle route and is at the layover stop in Eaton Road, near to Coventry railway station. (D. R. Harvey Collection)

526 (KRW 526F)

Opposite above: The last eight Commer BFD3023s all entered service during October 1967 and were identical to the two previous batches of Walker B12F-bodied buses. 526 (KRW 526F) is parked in Harnall Lane Garage. The buses had twin rear doors with very small van-type rear windows which revealed their origins all too clearly. Just before the West Midland PTE take over, all the seventeen Commers were transferred to Coventry District Council. Of the two front sliding doors, only the nearside one was equipped with handrails for the passengers while the offside one was solely for the use of the driver. (R. H. G. Simpson)

FGW 498C

Above: The AEC Swift was the first rear-engined AEC. Although it used similar side-members and steering gear as the slightly earlier Leyland Panther, it had AEC mechanical equipment and the newly introduced AH505 8.2-litre engine. The bus was fitted with a four-speed Monocontrol semi-automatic gearbox incorporating a fluid flywheel. The first Swift chassis was the MP2R chassis, which was bodied by Willowbrook with a B53F standard BET-style body and incorporated a single platform step and a flat, ramped floor. This bus was registered FGW 498C and used extensively by AEC as a demonstrator and it was used in Coventry during December 1965. Unfortunately, despite their lively performance, good fuel economy and quiet running, as with most of this first generation of full-sized, rear-engined buses, they suffered in normal service conditions from overheating and gearbox problems and many were withdrawn after quite short lives. FGW 498C is parked when still displaying its demonstration credentials in the front destination box. The bus was sold to Gelligaer UDC in 1967, becoming their 35. (D. R. Harvey Collection)

1 (CKV 1D)

Working on the 27 route to Toll Bar End is the first of the twenty-two East Lancs/
Neepsend-bodied Daimler Fleetline CRG6LXs. 1 (CKV 1D), standing outside the Priory
Restaurant, was bodied by Neepsend with a H45/31F seating layout. The bus is operating in
its original predominantly cream livery with a maroon roof and skirt with a band of the same
colour above the lower saloon windows, this being the same attractively bright arrangement
as the previous Atlanteans and Fleetlines. Neepsend was a subsidiary of Cravens of Sheffield,
whose body building operation was purchased by East Lancashire Coachbuilders of Blackburn.
Neepsend built buses solely to East Lancs designs from 1964 to 1968 and the only easy way to
identify any difference between the products of the two coachbuilders when they were new was
that the panel below the windscreen on the buses bodied by Neepsend was built in two pieces.
(A. J. Douglas)

3 (CKV 3D)

3 (CKV 3D) leaves Broadgate and is passing the Owen Owen department store in Trinity Street. It is working on the 16A route to Keresley Road. The bus is painted in the 1970 livery with the whole of the area below the lower saloon windows painted in Marshall Red. This hid the road mud much better than the previous cream, but looked somehow less adventurous. This Sandy Lane Garage-based Daimler Fleetline CRG6LX was one of thirteen of this batch of twenty-two buses bodied by Neepsend in Sheffield to the standard East Lancs design. The convoluted link between Cravens, their subsidiary Neepsend, named after the area in Sheffield in which the bodybuilder's factory was located, meant that bus bodies were once again briefly manufactured in the Steel City. This only lasted for four years before the Neepsend factory was closed because the quality of build of the Sheffield organisation products was considered to be not as good as the bodies manufactured in Blackburn. On the opposite side of the road is 31 (KWK 31F), another Daimler Fleetline CRG6LX but with an ECW body with front and centre doors. (M. Hayhoe)

4 (CKV 4D)

Above: A brand-new 4 (CKV 4D), a Daimler Fleetline CRG6LX with a Neepsend H45/31F body, along with CKV 1D, entered service in March 1966. It is displaying the 3 route destination for Stoke Aldermoor. These buses introduced curved windscreens into the bus fleet for the first time, which improved the appearance of the vehicles. The strange arrangement of deep sliding lower saloon ventilators and the tiny upper saloon ventilators was perhaps a little peculiar; this was when smoking in the upper saloon of buses was still allowed, when a thick fug of cigarette smoke really required good ventilation to clear the stale atmosphere. (D. R. Harvey Collection)

7 (CKV 7D)

Opposite above: The 1970 livery of Marshall Red and ivory somehow didn't 'look right' when applied to the East Lancashire-bodied Daimler Fleetlines as it accentuated the depth of the upper saloon windows. This Sandy Lane garaged bus is 7 (CKV 7D), which entered service in April 1966 and is operating on the 16A service to Keresley Road. It is loading up with passengers at the stop in front of the large Owen Owen store in Broadgate. The bus has been renumbered in the WMPTE series as 7Y but still retains the Coventry Transport fleet name. The triangular smoked glass staircase window had by now been replaced by a plain panel. (D. R. Harvey Collection)

13 (CKV 13D)

Above: Renumbered by WMPTE in 1979 as 1013, this was one of the Neepsend-bodied Daimler Fleetline CRG6LXs. Of the twenty-two members of the class numbered 1–22, thirteen were bodied by Neepsend while the remainder were constructed by East Lancs. All had a H45/31F seating layout. As regards merits of the build quality of the Coventry buses in this order, the withdrawal dates of the buses with Neepsend-built bodies compared to the East Lancs products do not provide conclusive data regarding longevity. Nine of the former were withdrawn in 1979 compared to seven of the East Lancs ones while the remainder were all withdrawn during the following year on a four to two basis. 13 was one of the four Neepsend-bodied buses withdrawn in 1980. It is loading up in Pool Meadow bus station in the full Oxford Blue and cream livery of the PTE when working on the by now renumbered 32 service to Tile Hill Village. (R. H. G. Simpson)

14 (CKV 14D)

Above: Travelling along Fairfax Street is a rather dirty-looking East Lancs-bodied 14 (CKV 14D). This bus is being used on the 27 Armstrong Whitworth works service to Bagington. On the far side of the road is Pool Meadow coach park and waiting there is a Red & White ECW-bodied Bristol RELH coach. The Coventry Transport Daimler Fleetline CRG6LX is about to turn right into Pool Meadow bus station, which even in the 1960s had far better facilities than the appallingly equipped transport interchange used by the long-distance coach operators. Just visible on the right is a Midland Red CM5 motorway coach which was about to leave this ash-covered, bleak spot for the almost luxurious delights of Victoria coach station in London. (L. Mason)

22 (CKV 22D)

Opposite below: During the rebuilding of Pool Meadow bus station, buses were parked where they could find a space. Behind the bus is Fairfax Street with its 1960s buildings, including the newly opened Sainsbury's multi-storey car park. 22 (CKV 22D), a Daimler Fleetline CRG6LX with an East Lancashire H44/31F body, is soon to operate on the 20 route to Bedworth. East Lancs built this style of double-deck body for both Warrington and Sheffield Corporation, with the latter on Leyland Atlantean chassis having the same curved, two-piece windscreen. This bus had a fourteen-year service life which was cut short by the introduction of fifteen new MCW Metrobus Mark Is to the Coventry fleet. Meanwhile, most of the Willowbrook-bodied Atlanteans and Fleetlines outlived most of the East Lancs bodies, suggesting that irrespective of them being bodied by either East Lancs themselves or Neepsend, they were not as durable as the slightly earlier rear-engined buses. (D. R. Harvey Collection)

18 (CKV 18D)

Above: The line of Austin FX4 taxi cabs is parked outside the mock Tudor-fronted Pool Meadow Café where they await customers, usually from the coach park off to the right. With the Swanswell Ringway elevated ring road in the background, 18 (CKV 18D) comes out of the bus station and approaches Fairfax Street when working on the 13 service to Willenhall. 18 was bodied by Neepsend and entered service in May 1966 and is painted in the Marshall Red and ivory livery of 1970 but has the West Midland PTE fleet names and the fleet number 18Y. (D. R. Harvey Collection)

HWU 641C

Above: The Bristol RELL6G was introduced in 1962 and was the first of the 1960s 36-foot-long, rear-engined chassis to enter production, though until 1965 all chassis were only available to the BTC Group of nationalised bus operators. The RELL was powered by a Gardner 6HLX 10.45-litre engine. HWU 641C was inspected by the management of Coventry Transport on 4 January 1966, prior to a week's operation in Birmingham. The bus had been built in late 1965 as West Yorkshire Road Car's SRG 15 and had an ECW B54F body with the original curved windscreen design and rounded rear dome. It stands in the turning circle outside the Weoley Castle public house in Shenley Lane, Northfield, on Saturday 15 January 1966 when demonstrating to Birmingham City Transport on their 20 route. The Bristol/Gardner combination created a favourable impression with Coventry's senior staff as it led to them ordering six of the shorter ECW-bodied RESL6Gs. (B. W. Ware)

516 (KHP 516E)

Opposite below: As a result of the demonstration of HWU 641C, Coventry Corporation was one of the first municipalities to buy Bristol/ECW buses after they became available on the open market; they bought six RESL-1s, which were delivered in 1967. These buses were the 32-foot, 6-inch-long version of the longer RELL with a service body with only five bays and a narrow front entrance. The two front destination boxes were in line with a small route number box above. A similar two-track service number blind was incorporated into the rear dome. Three, including 518, had forty-four-seat, single-doorway bodies while the other three had forty-two-seat, dual-doorway bodies. These buses were an interesting assortment of styles, with a flat and shallow windscreen and a very flat front with no overhang at all. The first of the two-door buses, 516 (KHP 516E), is parked at the edge of Pool Meadow bus station when new and equipped for one-man-operation. (J. C. Cockshott)

LAX 104E

Above: Between 6 and 14 April 1967, a Red & White-owned Bristol RESL6L, numbered RS4.67 in the Chepstow-based fleet, was borrowed as a demonstration vehicle, although the Coventry fleet had already received 516–521 two months earlier. This bus was the 33-foot-long version and had the original style of curved windscreen fitted to its ECW B46F body whereas the Coventry buses had the less attractive flat version, although LAX 104E had the same rounded rear dome. This is the next vehicle in the batch, RS5.67 (LAX 105E), working on the 178 route to Cardiff. (R. H. G. Simpson)

518 (KHP 518E)

Both the single-door and two-door buses were used on the CITY-RAILBUS service between the railway station and Pool Meadow having taken over from the pioneering Marshall-bodied Bedford VAS1s which, ironically, with only thirty seats were a victim of their own success. 518 (KHP 518E), a Bristol RESL1 with an ECW B44F body, leaves Station Approach at Coventry railway station. This bus had entered service in 1967 and was technically sold to West Midlands PTE prior to the take-over along with three others and became 4444. These six buses were due for their half-life recertification and, as there was a need for single-deckers in Wolverhampton, the six Bristol RESLs were quickly overhauled in March 1974. The four renumbered buses began operating in the Wolverhampton area within days of the Coventry Transport fleet's absorption. The final result was that the batch was renumbered in a rather confusing sequence as 516Y, 4443–4444, 519 (no Y suffix!) and 4445–4446. (A. J. Douglas)

519 (KHP 519E)

The first of the dual-doored trio of ECW-bodied Bristol RESL6Gs was 519 (KHP 519E), new in February 1967. These three buses had a reduced seating layout of forty-two but were otherwise the same as the single-doored three, having red moquette upholstered seating. Like the other buses, they were all initially used on the railway station to bus station 25 service. It is turning into Ironmonger's Row from Trinity Street when working on the 25 route. The bus has just passed the impressive mock Tudor buildings at the top of Trinity Street. In 1974, 519 was bought by WMPTE and it became their 4446. Eventually the complete batch of these six Bristol single-deckers was renumbered into one series once again; this occurred in September 1976 when they became 5516–5521. These buses had a Gardner 6HLX engine, and were ideal for city work, but gradually the complete batch became underused and redundant as their original work was taken over by double-deckers. (C. W. Routh)

24 (KWK 24F)

The return to the open market of the Lowestoft-based Eastern Coach Works quickly saw the company obtaining orders for their well-built if somewhat staid-looking bodywork. One of the first was a batch of eighteen Daimler Fleetlines with ECW dual-doorway bodies delivered in March and April 1968. They were among the first double-deckers in Britain to be designed, built and equipped for one-man-working from new. They carried the Monobus name on the nearside windscreen. The entire batch was converted to single doorway layout, retaining the centre staircases, in 1973/74, and passed to West Midlands PTE in that condition. The last two of these buses was withdrawn by the PTE in 1983. 24 (KWK 24F) stands in Sandy Lane Garage yard when apparently new but without its wheel nut guard rings. (D. R. Harvey Collection)

26 (KWK 26F)

Loading up in Broadgate in front of the soon to be demolished, twenty-five-year-old 'temporary' shops is 26 (KWK 26F). This ECW-bodied Daimler Fleetline CRG6LX is working on the 17 route, which had been curtailed to Fenside from Bagington in 1965 because of the difficulty in crossing the extremely busy A45 road. With the lack of push-out ventilators in the front upper-deck windows, and the roll-over ventilators in the upper saloon, the unfamiliar ECW bodies for the open market showed that the newly privatised company was prepared to meet the requirements of new municipal customers. However, the traditional ECW shape was still there, with the top deck still looking remarkably like the bodywork built on 'Lodekkas'. The offside of the bus reveals the centrally located staircase opposite the middle exit door. On their conversion to single-door, the staircase remained in the same position. Dominating this side of Broadgate is the fourteenth-century Perpendicular Gothic-styled west end of the nave of Holy Trinity Church. (Cotswold PSV Group)

30 (KWK 30F)

Above: Parked at the bus shelters in Pool Meadow bus station is Daimler Fleetline CRG6LX 30Y (KWK 30F), one of Sandy Lane Garage's vehicles. It is working on the 7 route to Allesley in about 1975. This Eastern Coach Works-bodied bus had already been repainted in WMPTE colours though the two buses in the distance, 13 (CKV 13D), with a Neepsend body, and the East Lancs-bodied 106 (YVC 106K), are still in Coventry's final livery. Towering over the bus station on the other side of Fairfax Street is the 211-room De Vere Hotel built in the late 1960s, with Coventry Cathedral's nave opposite on the extreme left. (A. J. Douglas)

31 (KWK 31F)

Opposite below: 31Y (KWK 31F) speeds into Broadgate from Trinity Street when operating the 25 route, which had only a few years earlier been the preserve of the thirty-seat Bedford VAS1s. For once, the Oxford Blue and cream livery of WMPTE actually enhanced the appearance of the ECW-bodied Fleetlines. Straddling the Coventry fleet's take-over by the PTE, during 1973 and 1974 their bodies were rebuilt with the centre door being removed. Although the centre staircase was retained, two extra seats were placed where the middle doors had been, thus increasing the seating capacity to H45/29F. Along with the rest of the surviving Coventry bus fleet, in December 1979 this bus had 1000 added to its fleet number, thus becoming 1031. In this guise this Sandy Lane-based bus was to remain in service until 1982. (PM Photography)

35 (KWK 35F)

Above: After November 1979, all the surviving Coventry buses were renumbered by 1000 being added to the existing fleet number and the Y suffix was dropped. Very late in its career the now renumbered 1035 (KWK 35F) is parked near the top of Trinity Street. It is apparently empty and awaiting its crew before operating on the Alderman's Green 31 service. These buses had their three destination boxes mounted higher than normal at basically the floor level of the upper saloon which, with the shallow windscreen and the deep front panel above it, did make for a somewhat untidy appearance emphasised by the WM blue and cream livery. (D. Savage)

39 (KWK 39F)

Above: Travelling along Far Gosford Street towards the bus station at Pool Meadow on 5 August 1971 is 39 (KWK 39F), which is being used on the 4 route from Wyken. This route was in the second tranche to be converted to one-man-operation in January 1970, when it was also extended to serve Walsgrave Hospital. Following the bus is a Leyland Super Comet flatbed lorry while the van on the left was owned by Herbert Copeland is a Morris J4 12 cwt. The bus was allocated to Harnall Lane Garage, as the H on the deep front Arabian maroon band shows. This garage identifier was introduced in about 1969. (C. W. Routh)

36 (KWK 36F)

Opposite above: The bus used for the official photograph of the 23–40 class of Eastern Coach Works-bodied Daimler Fleetline CRG6LXs was 36 (KWK 36F). The bus was delivered to Coventry Corporation in April 1968 and these eighteen buses were the first buses in the fleet to be equipped for one-man-operation. The thick middle maroon band at the front of the bus and the shallow windscreen were the least attractive features of the body design. It was noticeable that the front doors were mounted lower than the middle ones and were also wider, allowing for cash paying and pass carrying passengers to be served by the driver while everyone else boarded on the right-hand side of the entrance. (ECW)

41 (KKV 41G)

Above: The next order for eighteen buses was again for Daimler Fleetline CRG6LXs but the body contract returned to East Lancashire. They were again two-door with central exits and a revised and much improved frontal appearance. They all had a H45/27D seating layout but 41 was converted to H44/29F in February 1975. The first of these buses, 41 (KKV 41G), turns from Bishop Street into King Street when working on the 15 route to Whitmore Park on 21 June 1972. Crossing Hales Street is a Midland Red D9 double-decker and a 36-foot-long S23 single-decker while in the distant Burges is the large mid-1950s Owen Owen department store. (E. V. Trigg)

42 (KKV 42G)

Above: Coventry Cathedral's original medieval fourteenth-century tower and spire was the only complete part of St Michael's to have survived the bombing of 14/15 November 1940 but, along with the tower and spire of Holy Trinity parish church, frame the Coventry skyline and overlook Pool Meadow bus station on the other side of Fairfax Street. The new cathedral had already been completed and consecrated but the De Vere Hotel had yet to be built, although Sainsbury's car park with its concrete fretwork sides had been opened. 42 (KKV 42G), a Daimler Fleetline CRG6LX with a two-door East Lancs body, brightens up the scene in its predominantly ivory livery, making the following Daimler CVG6 look dowdy in comparison. The centre exit door on these bodies was placed in the middle body bay with the staircase directly opposite. (A. J. Douglas)

46 (KKV 46G)

Opposite below: Two of the Daimler Fleetline CRG6LXs delivered in January 1969 with an East Lancashire H45/27D body and a central staircase positioned directly opposite the exit doors leave Pool Meadow bus station in 1970. 46 (KKV 46G) is working on the 5A service to Coundon while 52 (KKV 52G) is leaving on the 4 route to Walsgrave Hospital. Both buses are quite well laden after a hard day's work and could do with a session in a garage bus wash. Both buses would be converted to an H44/29F in 1974 and 1975 respectively. The policy of converting dual-door Fleetlines was instigated by the Corporation and was continued by WMPTE as the drivers of one-man-operated buses occasionally had difficulty in seeing clearly the centre doors when passengers were crowding around them prior to alighting. Accidents and even a small number of fatalities had occurred and this resulted in a much-needed change of policy and a reversion to only front entrances so the safe movement of passengers could be easily monitored. (L. Mason)

45 (KKV 45G)

Above: Waiting at the traffic lights in Corporation Street at the junction with the Burges is 45 (KKV 45G). This two-door, East Lancs-bodied Daimler Fleetline CRG6LX entered service in January 1969 and was within a year of this date when it was working on the 2 route to Cheylesmore. The deep windscreen certainly improved both the appearance of the bus and the visibility from the driver's cab and front platform. Behind the bus is the mock Tudor frontage of the mid-Victorian Wine Lodge public house, which was tied to the east London-based Truman's Brewery. The Sandy Lane allocated bus is equipped for one-man-operation with instructions for intending passengers above the front entrance on how to board the vehicle. (F. W. York)

49 (KKV 49G)

The multi-storey De Vere Hotel towers above Pool Meadow bus station as 49Y (KKV 49G) stands parked just short of its loading stop while the driver takes a break. The bus is bound for Coundon and has been repainted in the PTE livery of blue and cream. This style of East Lancs body with the peaked front and rear domes, on a Daimler Fleetline CRG6LX for the first time, topped 1 hundredweight over 9 tons, a far cry from when the first of the RWK-registered Daimler CVG6s weighed exactly 2 tons less. This style of body was supplied to numerous municipal operators, appearing on Leyland Atlantean, Daimler Fleetline, Bristol VR and lastly Dennis Dominator chassis. The 5 route had been introduced in June 1928 and started outside the Coventry Hippodrome before heading westwards via Jordan Well, High Street, Smithford Street and Coundon Road to Barkers' Butts Lane. Its city terminus was only moved into the bus station after the rebuilding of Pool Meadow. (L. Mason)

53 (KKV 53G)

Travelling through the eastern side of Broadgate from Trinity Street is 53 (KKV 53G). The large Owen Owen department store dominates the north side of the square, which in 1970 still allowed through running into High Street. The bus, a brand-new Daimler Fleetline CRG6LX with an East Lancs body, is working on the 16A service and would go all the way round Broadgate before reaching its terminus on the opposite side of the square in front of the Leofric Hotel. It would then head out to the north-west of the city along Keresley Road via Ironmonger Row and The Burges. (C. W. Routh)

56 (KKV 56G)

Above: Renumbered in November 1979 along with all of the surviving Coventry Transport bus fleet, the driver of 1056 (KKV 56G) makes a spirited exit from the bus station when taking a nearly full load of passengers on the 32 service to Potters Green, a residential suburb situated in the north-east of the city. This route subsequently was renumbered 8. This East Lancs-bodied Daimler Fleetline CRG6LX had been rebuilt from the original H45/27D layout to a H44/29F configuration by the removal of the central exit door in May 1975. It is therefore surprising that 1056 only ran for barely five years in this form before it was withdrawn. (R. H. G. Simpson)

59 (SWK 59J)

Opposite above: The next contract for bus bodies was won by Park Royal and they were the heaviest buses delivered thus far to Coventry Transport. The bodies on the Daimler Fleetline CRG6LX chassis had a H45/27D seating layout and weighed 9 tons 3 cwt and, while retaining the central staircase and exit door configuration, the whole of this structural section was moved forward by one bay. The body style had much larger saloon windows, being 5 feet 4 inches long, some 15 inches longer than those on the East Lancashire bodies and resulting in an improved four-bay body style. It entered service in September 1970 and was similar in style to the 33-foot-long bodies ordered by Birmingham and Wolverhampton Corporations and delivered to WMPTE. 59 (SWK 59J) works across the Burges junction from Hales Street into Corporation Street on the 3 route in 1974 in full West Midlands livery. (D. R. Harvey Collection)

62 (SWK 62J)

Above: Operating on the 2 route to Radford with a conductor is 62 (SWK 62J). The bus is loading up with passengers in front of the Owen Owen store in Broadgate. 62 was delivered in September 1970 in yet another variation of the Marshall Red and Shetland Ivory livery. The outline of the Park Royal body was similar to the contemporary 4036–4135 batch of Daimler Fleetlines ordered by the newly formed West Midlands PTE. The central staircase and exit doors and the deep windscreen considerably altered the appearance of these Coventry Transport buses and, when they were transferred to Selly Oak Garage in Birmingham, they looked like a shorter version of the 33-foot-long 'Jumbos' which were being prematurely withdrawn due to structural failures around the central platform. (D. R. Harvey Collection)

65 (SWK 65J)

Above: One of the last, almost defiant, livery variations before the West Midlands take-over was the placing of the Coventry municipal crest above the front destination boxes and retaining the Coventry Transport fleet name on the lower side panels. 65 (SWK 65J), a seventy-two-seat Park Royal-bodied Daimler Fleetline CRG6LX, is working on the 30 route to Bedworth and is standing in the same corner of Broadgate as bus 62 in the previous photograph. Next to it is the sign for Alexandre, the gentleman's bespoke tailors who occupied the premises near to the Owen Owen store. (D. R. Harvey Collection)

70 (SWK 70J)

Opposite below: Painted in West Midlands PTE blue and cream, 70 (SWK 70J) was the only one of the eighteen Park Royal-bodied, dual-door Daimler Fleetline CRG6LXs to be converted to a single-door layout. The middle door was taken out in August 1975, but it did not re-enter service until March 1976. In its rebuilt state, 70 failed to meet the Construction and Use Regulations on staircase and gangway clearances. As a result the lower saloon seating capacity was reduced to only twenty-four, which was economically too few to make further conversions viable. The result was that the bus looked even more like a standard WMPTE XON-J, YOX-K registered Park Royal-bodied Daimler Fleetline. The bus is in Hales Street and is opposite the Coventry Theatre when working on the 21 route on Tuesday 7 October 1980. (F. W. York)

72 (SWK 72J)

Above: The driver of 72 (SWK 72J) appears to be having 'a little tootle' around Pool Meadow bus station on 26 October 1971, although in reality he is probably manoeuvring the bus to a bus stance or even just leaving the bus station in order to return to its garage, in this case Sandy Lane. The bus is painted with the passenger instructions over the front door and is still basically in as-delivered condition. It was perhaps surprising that Coventry did not order any more Park Royal bodies, though by about 1972 the Southall-based coachbuilder was beginning to build large orders for London Transport and had a rather full order book. (A. J. Douglas)

75 (SWK 75J)

Park Lane Garage's 75 (SWK 75J) stands empty when working on the 15 route to Green Lane.
It is parked in front of the 'temporary' pre-fab shops on the east side of Broadgate. These were
built in the first early post-war years and were demolished in March 1974. 75 (SWK 75J), the
penultimate Park Royal dual-door-bodied Daimler Fleetline CRG6LX, is in the Marshall Red
and Shetland Ivory livery. The Marshall Red colour was not a reference to Russian military
parades in Red Square, but to Bert Marshall who was Coventry Transport's foreman painter in
the 1960s, who introduced this brownish red colour to the bus fleet. (D. R. Harvey Collection)

76 (SWK 76J)

76 (SWK 76J), in WMPTE livery, turns into Swanswell Street when working on the 22 route to Willenhall. The bus is seen passing the late-Victorian public house that had opened as the Board Vaults in 1896 and was demolished in 1999, having survived as the Swanswell Hotel since 1904. 76 led an eventful early life. It was exhibited at the 1970 Commercial Motor Show with its original Park Royal H45/27D body. Its body was destroyed by fire in April 1971, and the chassis was salvaged. A new single-door East Lancashire H44/30F body was added to the 95–122 order and fitted to 76 in March 1972. (W. J. Haynes)

77 (YHP 477J)

Above: The first of the YHP-registered buses was 77 (YHP 477J), an East Lancs-bodied
Daimler Fleetline which was delivered in May 1971 and, like all Coventry's buses since 1968,
was equipped for one-man-operation from new. Built with two doors, 77 was converted to
front entrance only in November 1977 and reseated as a result of the removal of the centre
exit to H44/29F. A somewhat despairing passenger in the lower saloon looks hopefully for the
driver to turn up in order to take the bus out of Pool Meadow bus station on the renumbered
8A service, formerly the 21 service, to Bell Green. The bus is carrying an advertisement for
British Caledonian, an airline which operated from Gatwick airport from 1970 until 1988.
(A. J. Douglas)

80 (YHP 480J)

Opposite above: Parked on the Fairfax Street side of Pool Meadow bus station is East
Lancs-bodied Daimler Fleetline CRG6LX 80 (YHP 480J). At last the Coventry Transport
manager specified a large single-aperture destination blind, which was an improvement on the
earlier three separate front boxes. Converted to single-door layout in 1978, it was renumbered
1080 along with the rest of the fleet in November 1979 and it is in this guise it awaits its next
duty on the 35 route. The advertisement on the side panel of 1080 reads: 'Shakespeare would
have written better with a Berol,' but unfortunately school children, to whom they were largely
supplied to in schools, didn't! (B. J. Whitelaw)

84 (YHP 484J)

Above: On 26 October 1971, Daimler Fleetline CRG6LX 84 (YHP 484J) pulls away from the 5A route bus shelter and begins its tight U-turn to pass in front of the half-timbered Meadow Café and then to the Fairfax Street exit. The centre exit door on these East Lancs bodies was in the second bay and was, because of the bodybuilder's five-bay construction and short-length saloon windows, even further forward than on previous dual-door bodies. Although the buses had a single-step entrance, there was a substantial step into the lower saloon and as a consequence, the centre exit had two steps. The new location of the centre door was in order to allow the driver of the one-man bus to have a better view over the area at the bottom of the staircase. Significantly, WMPTE did not like the centre doors on Coventry's rear-engined buses and 84 was converted to H44/29F in December 1977. (A. J. Douglas)

85 (YHP 485J)

Above: Carrying the MONOBUS Perspex plate in the nearside windscreen, the one-man-operated 85 (YHP 485J) travels out of the city on the 18 route to Canley, passing a well patronised children's playground with numerous swings and slides. The almost new Daimler Fleetline CRG6LX has an East Lancashire H45/27D body and was new in June 1971. The bus was converted to H44/29F in February 1978. The 18 route was first operated by the Corporation in April 1936, when it was acquired from Bunty Motorways. It travelled south-westwards out of the city via Spon Street, Spon End, Hearsall Lane to Canley Road. (R. F. Mack)

96 (YVC 96K)

Opposite below: The vinyl WM WEST MIDLANDS logo on the side of the bus had been applied on 1 April 1974 when the PTE took over the Corporation's transport operations. The sticker had a Marshall Red ground and until the proper transfers could be applied, this was a quick way to show the new ownership. 96Y (YVC 96K) was the second of the large order for twenty-eight further Daimler Fleetline CRG6LXs whose delivery began in March 1972. The body order once more went to the Blackburn-based coach builder East Lancashire, but for the first time since the 1–22 numbered buses of 1966, these vehicles reverted to a single front entrance with a H44/30F layout. 96 is standing in the bus station at Pool Meadow. (D. R. Harvey Collection)

PNF 941L

Above: A Leyland Atlantean was demonstrated to Coventry Transport for a month between 26 June and 23 July 1971. This was a PDR1A/1, with a Northern Counties H43/22F body which was numbered EX1 in the SELNEC PTE fleet. It was painted in their garish orange and white livery, which looked attractive when freshly painted but subsequently weathered quite badly after a comparatively short time in service. The bus was four months old when it was demonstrated to Coventry and used on the 16 service to Keresley Road. It was obviously not a success as no orders were placed for the Atlantean chassis as a result of the visit of EX1. (A. J. Douglas)

103 (YVC 103K)

The end of the road! Dumped in Adderley Street garage yard in March 1986 is 103 (YVC 103K), now renumbered 1103. In order to prevent the bus 'escaping' the scrapman's acetylene torch, the PTE removed the bulky Gardner 10.45-litre engine for resale and then cut off the rear chassis extension, thus rendering the bus inoperable. A similar job had been done on the Metro-Cammell-bodied Bristol VRT sitting in the mud to the front of 1103. The fleet names and legal ownership had been removed and normally the fleet number would have been painted over, but 1103 has been dignified by the retention of its fleet number. (D. R. Harvey)

105 (YVC 105K)

Broadgate was the alternative hub for buses terminating in the city centre and remained so until the square was all but removed in 1990. The 21 route to Wood End had its terminus in front of the Leofric Hotel and the entrance to the famous 1950s Precinct, which was built in a mellow red brick and when it was opened was the country's first pedestrianised shopping precinct. The driver of Daimler Fleetline 105 (YVC 105K) has a quick look at his newspaper before readying himself for the next load of passengers. The paintwork on the East Lancs bodywork still looks new on this bus that was delivered in May 1972 and as 1105 it would remain in service as one of the last of the class until 1986. (J. C. Walker)

111 (YVC 111K)

Above: By the late spring of 1978, all the 6721–6760 East Lancs-bodied Fleetlines were at Coventry after the first twenty's sojourn at Acocks Green Garage in Birmingham. Behind 111 (YVC 111K), which is pulling away from its stop in Trinity Street when working on the 2 route and is about to enter Broadgate, are two of these forty buses that were originally ordered by Coventry Transport. They are 6740 (NOC 740R), freshly returned to Coventry, and 6755 (SDA 755S). These were the only East Lancs-bodied Daimler Fleetline CRG6LXs to have ventilators in the upper saloon front windows and therefore could easily be identified. Since 1938, the buildings in the lower part of Trinity Street which had survived the blitz and the mock half-timbered Priory Gate had hardly changed. (M. Wood)

114 (YVC 114K)

Opposite above: Still in Coventry Transport's Marshall Red and ivory livery, 114 (YVC 114K) has the West Midlands vinyl fleet names and legal lettering on the lower saloon side panels covering any sign of the former municipal ownership. This one-man-operated MONOBUS working on the 17 service to Wyken is seen leaving Pool Meadow bus station at exactly 1:00 p.m. and passes the Meadow Café which, as it is lunch time, is doing a good trade in mugs of tea or coffee, meat pies and chips, fish and chips, sausage egg and chips, baked beans and chips, spam and chips, more chips. Sounds more like Monty Python, but it did a roaring trade and was only lost when the bus station went through yet another metamorphosis. It had huge CAFÉ lettering painted on the roof tiles, making it look somewhat like a seaside beach hut. (A. J. Douglas)

121 (YVC 121K)

Above: 121 (YVC 121K) overtakes 117 (YVC 117K) at the top of Trinity Street, when the road layout had been changed again with railings dividing the carriageways. Both buses are part of the contract for twenty-eight Daimler Fleetline CRG6LXs with East Lancs H44/30F bodywork and entered service in May 1972. 121 is being used on the 17 route to Fenside Avenue alongside the main A45 and is about to enter Broadgate. The 17 route had been cut back from its original Baginton terminus in 1965 because of the upgrading of the A45 Stonebridge Highway, which made the crossing of the new dual carriageway extremely difficult. 117 is standing empty at the 2 route bus stop when working to Cheylesmore. (A. J. Douglas)

407 (YVC 407L)

In August 1972 a single 36-foot-long coach, 407 (YVC 407L), was purchased as a replacement for the three 1964 Duple-bodied Bedford SB5s for use on excursions and private hire work. This was a Ford R226 powered by a Ford 140 bhp, front-mounted, underfloor engine coupled to a six-speed synchromesh gearbox. A Plaxton Panorama Elite C49F body was fitted, which was quite an improvement over the Bedfords. The Ford chassis was, compared to the contemporary AEC Reliance, Leyland Leopard and the recently introduced Volvo B58, a somewhat lighter chassis and it competed with the Bedford YRQ for this share of the market. Both manufacturers' products tended to have quite short, if productive, lives and so it was with 407. It was transferred to the West Midlands fleet and survived as the PTE's only coach until 1979, when it was withdrawn. It is parked on the forecourt of Quinton Garage, Birmingham, in 1980 awaiting sale and indeed it was sold to Carter of Litcham in the Breckland area of central Norfolk. (D. R. Harvey)

VWD 452H

In April 1972 VWD 452H, the second of two prototype Scania BR110Ms, was briefly demonstrated to Coventry Transport. This bus was the two-doored model and was bodied by MCW with a body style that had a distinctly Scandinavian appearance. The body had an asymmetrical windscreen arrangement, which was continued on the Metropolitan double-decker as well as the later Mark I Metrobus. VWD 452H is being demonstrated to Newport Corporation, who subsequently purchased forty-four of the type despite the sparkling performance being spoilt by having a poor level of fuel economy. No orders were placed by Coventry! (D. R. Harvey Collection)

124 (PDU 124M)

Below: 124 (PDU 124M) is about to pull away at the traffic lights at the exit from Pool Meadow bus station and turn into Fairfax Street when working on the 3 service to Stoke Aldermoor. This East Lancs-bodied Daimler Fleetline entered service in September 1973. These buses to some extent had their working lives curtailed and lasted in service for barely twelve years. This was not because the East Lancs product was not well built but rather mainly due to the PTE wishing to standardise on bodies built by MCW and Park Royal on Daimler Fleetline chassis. (D. R. Harvey Collection)

408 (YVC 408L)

Opposite above: 408 (YVC 408L) is parked over the pits in Sandy Lane Garage on 27 July 1981. The vehicle was a twelve-seater Ford Transit fitted with a 43 bhp Perkins 4/108 diesel engine which was too long to fit under the Transit's stubby nose, and so a longer bonnet was fitted. It was also quite an unpopular power unit as in 1974 it was replaced by Ford's own diesel power plant. Perhaps it is therefore no coincidence that the minibus has its engine out. 408 was bought as cover for the Commer minibuses delivered to Coventry Transport during the 1960s, all of which were transferred to Coventry's Social Services at the take-over of the municipal bus fleet, which occurred on 1 April 1974. In all probability, after a few years of service 408 became the garage 'hack', being used mainly for staff transport, and was withdrawn later in 1981. (D. R. Harvey Collection)

129 (GWK 129L)

Above: Compared to when they were first delivered in the full Coventry livery, the West Midlands PTE livery did nothing to enhance the looks of the East Lancs bodywork. When compared to the Mark II MCW Metrobus behind, it which had the lower saloon windows surrounds painted blue with a cream band between these windows and the lower blue panels, the vast area of cream above the lower saloon windows made these buses appear tall and a bit slab-like. 129 (GWK 129L) waits at Stand E in Pool Meadow bus station in March 1985 when working on the 6 route to Kingsbury Road. Behind it to the right is the large De Vere Hotel with the Coventry university halls of residence to the left and between them the tower of the old Coventry Cathedral. (D. R. Harvey)

135 (PDU 135M)

Above: The newest Coventry Transport bus to be preserved is 135 (PDU 135M). This Daimler
Fleetline CRG6LX with an East Lancashire H44/30F body entered service in September 1973
as one of the last six buses to be delivered to Coventry Transport and was withdrawn in 1986.
The class of twenty buses had their suffix letters split between L and M as six of the buses
were delivered two months after the rest of the group and after the August year registration
change-over. 135 is in the Aston Manor Bus Museum car park in Witton, opposite Aston Villa's
famous Villa Park, on 11 July 2010. (D. R. Harvey)

140 (PDU 140M)

Opposite below: 140 (PDU 140M), a Daimler Fleetline CRG6LX with an East Lancs H44/30F
body, turns into Little Park Street from High Street having been renumbered by WMPTE as
140Y. This bus was numerically the last bus delivered to the undertaking in September 1973, but
not the last member of the batch. It is being used on the 15 service to Green Lane. Behind the bus
is the Tudor-styled Council House. This was built in red sandstone and with its gables, leaded
bay windows and impressively arched entrance looked very imposing and a testament to civic
pride. The Council House was completed in 1917 and was opened on 11 June 1920 by the Duke
of York. (W. J. Haynes)

138 (GWK 138L)

Above: Leaving Pool Meadow bus station is 138 (GWK 138L), on the 27 route to Toll Bar End. To the right of the bus is the prefabricated Beech Tree Café, which was opposite the better known and much older Meadow Café. This café always had tables and chairs outside under a canopy for use in the summer months. Behind the bus is the travel information and booking office for the Red House Coach Group at the entrance to the coach park. 138 is a Daimler Fleetline CRG6LX with an East Lancs body and has been renumbered 138Y and has West Midlands fleet names attached to the Coventry maroon-painted lower panels. (R. F. Mack)

142 (GWK 142L)

The last of the final twenty buses delivered to Coventry Transport was numbered 142 (GWK 142L), but was delivered in June 1973 in advance of the last six M-registered buses. Still in Coventry's livery, the bus is parked in the bus station when renumbered 142Y. In the nearside windscreen, next to the Perspex MONOBUS sign, is the round orange electrical sign showing that the bus was equipped with a two-way radio. This Harnall Lane allocated bus is working on the 27 route to Toll Bar End. The nice tradition of having a DAIMLER badge on the front panel was maintained to the end as if to show the Corporation's loyalty to supporting local industry. (D. R. Harvey Collection)

Buses Ordered by Coventry Transport but Delivered to West Midlands PTE

4449 (ROK 449M)

4447–4466 were twenty standard Coventry specification East Lancashire-bodied Daimler Fleetline CRG6LXs. They were delivered to WMPTE in their full blue and cream livery from between July and September 1974. All were withdrawn in 1986 after comparatively short lives. Working on the 2 route to Radford just before Christmas 1982 is 4449 (ROK 449M). It is in Broadgate in front of the Leofric Hotel and is standing in front of 6984 (WDA 984T), a standard Leyland Fleetline FE30AGR with a MCW H43/33F body that was delivered in December 1978. (M. Wood)

4461 (ROK 461M)

Travelling into Birmingham city centre in Digbeth when crossing the junction with Moat Row is 4461 (ROK 461M). On Monday 13 April 1981 it is working on the 959 express service from Coventry, though perhaps typically at this time it is not displaying any destination details. Behind the East Lancs-bodied Daimler Fleetline while it turns right into Meriden Street in front of the Smithfield Garage is a Mini Clubman and a Ford Capri. The bus is carrying a full load of passengers, which is not surprising as this was a Labour Party inspired promotional Mondays-only 'Funday' service which ran between 2 March and 8 June 1981. A flat fare of 10p for adults and 5p for children resulted in a lot of joy riders and a loss of revenue of £1.5 million. (F. W. York)

4466 (TOE 466N)
Parked outside Sainsbury's supermarket in Trinity Street is Daimler Fleetline CRG6LX 4466 (ROK 466M). It is being used on the 15 route to Whitmore Park on 27 July 1981, a service that had a daily headway of 15 minutes. The bus is one of the batch of East Lancs buses ordered by Coventry Transport and delivered to WMPTE. It was allocated to Sandy Lane Garage. When compared to the standard Metro-Cammell-bodied Fleetline parked behind it, the five-bay East Lancs bodywork looks distinctly fussy and somewhat old-fashioned. (D. R. Harvey Collection)

Below: **6741 (NOC 741R)**

Waiting in St Paul's bus station on 30 January 1997, in its twilight months of service, is 6726 (NOC 726R). This East Lancs-bodied Leyland Fleetline FE30AGR is working on the 329 service to Blakenhall when owned by the privatised Travel West Midlands. It was allocated to Birchills Garage for only a few months prior to its withdrawal. The bus is painted in the blue and silver livery with a broad red stripe. This was about the third reincarnation of St Paul's bus station, when the bus stands were rearranged diagonally. (D. R. Harvey)

6722 (NOC 722R)

Opposite above: Turning in front of the row of 1920s buildings in the centre of Acocks Green in order to park at the return terminus outside the New Inns public house on 5 May 1977 is 6722 (NOC 722R). It is working on the 1 service, which went on a meandering route into Birmingham's city centre via Springfield, Moseley and Edgbaston. Although the East Lancashire bodies were modified to WMPTE specification, these Leyland Fleetline FE30AGRs were quite clearly a bus ordered by the former Coventry Transport municipal undertaking. These buses had the distinctive lower mounted first bay alongside the front entrance and an almost standard front destination box. The bus was one of the first twenty of the class initially allocated to Acocks Green Garage in Birmingham in the spring of 1977, when there was union action over the further introduction of one-man-operation in Coventry. These East Lancs-bodied Leyland Fleetline F30AGRs added a touch of variety on the routes operated by Acocks Green Garage, where they remained for just over a year before going to Coventry. (E. V. Trigg)

6755 (SDA 755S)

Above: 6755 (SDA 755S) stands in Pool Meadow bus station when working on the 3 service to Holbrooks. These buses were equipped with opening upper saloon front windows and the dropped alignment of the front nearside saloon window was installed in order for the buses to have a nearside route number box. In addition, the lower saloon panels were split with a chrome strip in order to create a lower skirt panel; this enabled damaged lower panels to be replaced at a much lower cost and, as a by-product, enhanced the appearance of the buses. This was one of the last twenty of the class that were delivered when new to Coventry. (P. Yeomans)

Coventry Transport Bus Fleet 1948–1974

Fleet Nos	Registration Nos	Chassis	Chassis Nos	Body	Seating	Modifications/ Notes	Years In	Years Out
	GNE 247	Crossley DD42/1	93901	Crossley	H28/26R	Post war Crossley double-decker demonstrator. Manchester CTD 1217	1946	1946
1–30	FHP 1–30	Daimler CVA6	12693-9/ 13268–73/ 13421–33/ 14395–6/ 13434/94	MCCW	H31/29R		1948	1964–66
31–96	GKV 31–96	Daimler CVA6	14397–418/ 21–24/ 19–20/ 25–61/13267	MCCW	H31/29R		1949–50/52	1962–68
97–98	GKV 97–98	Daimler CVD6	12692/14393	MCCW	H31/29R		1950–51	1964–65
99	GKV 99	AEC Regent III 0961RT	0961217	MCCW	H30/26R	LTE 3RT7 type	1951	1964
100	GKV 100	Crossley DD42/7T	94940	MCCW	H31/27R	Painted in reverse livery	1951	1965
101–108	GKV 101–108	Daimler CVD6	14462–9	Brush	B34F		1949	1963–64
109–116	HKV 109–116	Daimler CVD6	14689–96	Brush	B34F		1949	1963–67
117–125	JKV 117–125	Maudslay Regent III M9612E	M9612E 4639–47	MCCW	H31/27R		1951	1964–65
126–165	KVC 126–165	Daimler CVD6	17298–318/ 331/19–24/27/ 333/25–6/28–31/34–7	MCCW	H31/27R	BCT 'New Look' front	1951–52	1965–72
	MOF 132	Daimler CVG6	18226	Crossley	H30/25R	On hire from BCT 3132	1953	1953
	REH 500	Daimler CLG5	18334	MCCW	H32/26R	On hire from PMT 500	1953	1953
	7194 H	AEC Regent III	U163966	Park Royal	H32/26R	AEC demonstrator	1953	1953
166–190	RWK 166–190	Daimler CVG6	18793–18894/81–93	MCCW	H33/27R		1955–56	1971–72
191–215	SKV 191–215	Daimler CVG6	19135–59	MCCW	H33/27R		1956–57	1972–77
	SDU 711	Daimler CVG6	18954	Willowbrook	H37/29R D		1956	1956
	VKV 99	Daimler CVG6/30	30001	Willowbrook	H41/33R		1957	1957
216–265	VWK 216–265	Daimler CVG6	19460–84/92–516	MCCW	H33/27R		1958	1970–78
401–403	XRW 401–403	Daimler Freeline D650H/S	25710–2	Willowbrook	C41F		1959	1970
266–290	XVC 266–290	Daimler CVG6	19646–70	MCCW	H33/27R	281 CVD6	1959	1977–78
291–312	291–312 RW	Daimler CVG6	19818–39	MCCW	H34/29R		1961	1973–78

	7000 HP	Daimler Fleetline CRG6LX	60000	Weymann	H44/33F	Daimler demonstrator	1962	1962
	SGD584	Leyland Atlantean PR1/1	620827	Alexander	H44/34F	Leyland demonstrator. On hire from Glasgow LA6	1962	1962
313–337	313–337 CRW	Daimler CVG6	20024–48	MCCW	H34/29R		1963–	1978–79
404–406	404 CWK/ CDU 405–6B	Bedford SB5	94770/94940/44	Duple	C41F		1964	1972
501	CDU 51B	Ford Thames 530E	L30C852237K	Martin Walker	B25F		1964	1972
338–359	CDU 338–359S	Leyland Atlantean PDR1/2	L21338–359	Willowbrook	H44/32F		1965	1978–80
360–381	CRW 360–381C	Daimler Fleetline CRG6LX	61117–138	Willowbrook	H44/32F		1965	1978–80
502–508	CRW 502–508C	Bedford VAS1	1954/70/73/56/88/94–5	Marshall	B30F		1965	1968–73
509–515	CRW 509–515C	Commer BFD 3023	003267/88/3309/15–8	Walker	B12F	To Coventry DC 1974	1965	1974
	CRH 175C	Leyland Panther PSUR1/1	L24711	Roe	B44D	Leyland demonstrator. On hire from K-u-Hull Corp. 175	1965	1965
	FGW 498C	AEC Swift MP2R	MP2R001	Willowbrook	B53F	AEC demonstrator	1965	1965
1–22	CKV 1–22D	Daimler Fleetline CRG6LX	61721–42	Neepsend 1–5/9–11/13/16–18/22. East Lancs 6–8/12/14–15/9–21.	H45/31F		1966	1979–81
522–523	KDU 522–523D	Commer BFD 3023	003857/73	Walker	B12F	To Coventry DC 1966 1974	1966	1974
	HWU 641C	Bristol RELL6G	222103	ECW	B54F	Bristol demonstrator As West Yorks SRG 15	1966	1966
516–518	KHP 516–518E	Bristol RESL6G	RESL1/101–3	ECW	B44F		1967	1978–9
519–521	KHP 519–521E	Bristol RESL6G	RESL1/104–6	ECW	B42D		1967	1978
524–531	KRW 524–531F	Commer BFD 3023	004065–72	Walker	B12F	To Coventry DC 1974	1967	1974
	LAX 104E	Bristol RESL6L	RESL1/128	ECW	B46F	Bristol demonstrator Red & White RS4.67	1967	1967
23–40	KWK 23–40F	Daimler Fleetline CRG6LX	62633–50	ECW	H45/27D	All rebuilt to H44/28F.	1968	1982–83
41–58	KKV 41–58G	Daimler Fleetline CRG6LX	63111–28	East Lancs	H45/27D	All rebuilt to H44/29D	1969	1981–82
59–76	SWK 59–76J	Daimler Fleetline CRG6LX	64059–76	Park Royal	H45/27D	70 to H44/24F 76 rebodied East Lancs H44/30F 1972.	1970	1980–83
77–94	YHP 477–494J	Daimler Fleetline CRG6LX	64077–94	East Lancs	H45/27D	All rebuilt to H44/29F	1971	1983–85
	PNF 941J	Leyland Atlantean PDR1A/1	7003009	NCME	H43/22F	Leyland demonstrator. SENEC PTE EX1	1971	1971
95–122	YVC 95–122K	Daimler Fleetline CRG6LX	66045–72	East Lancs	H44/30F		1972	1985–86
407	YVC 407L	Ford R226	BCO4MA49961	Plaxton	C49F		1972	1982

	VWD 452H	Scania BR110M	541051	MCW	B31D	MCW demonstrator	1972	1972
408	GWK 408L	Ford Transit	BD05NJ55866	Deansgate	B12F		1973	1981
123–142	PDU 123–5M/GWK 126–32L/ PDU 133M/ GWK 134L/ PDU135M/G WK 136–	Daimler Fleetline CRG6LX	67445–463/ 67363	East Lancs	H44/30F		1973	1985–1986

	9L/PDU 40M/GWK 141–2L							
4447–4466	ROK 457–461M/TOE 462–66M	Daimler Fleetline CRG6LX	various	East Lancs	H44/30F	Ordered by Coventry. Delivered to WMPTE	1974	
6721–6760	NOC 721–745R/SDA74 6–760S	Daimler Fleetline CRG6LX	various	East Lancs	H44/33F	Ordered by Coventry. Delivered to WMPTE	1977–78	